Fly Fishing the Henry's Fork

Fly Fishing
the
Henry's Fork

by Mike Lawson and Gary LaFontaine

THE LYONS PRESS
Guilford, Connecticut
An imprint of The Globe Pequot Press

The Lyons Press is an imprint of The Globe Pequot Press.

Originally published by Greycliff Publishing Company.

The Library of Congress Cataloging-Publication Data is available on file.

Printed in the United States of America

ISBN 1-58574-506-5

10 9 8 7 6 5 4 3 2 1

To all the staff and directors past and present, and other members of the Henry's Fork Foundation who, with their hard work, sweat, and passion, have worked tirelessly to understand, restore, and protect the greatest of trout rivers.

CONTENTS

Preface . . . .*ix*

Map . . . .*xi*

Introduction *1*

CHAPTER 1   Sections of the River 6

Henry's Lake, Home of the Big Brookies 6

Henry's Lake Outlet 10

Coffee Pot Area 12

Island Park Reservoir 14

Box Canyon 17

    Stone Flies in the Box Canyon 21

    High Water in the Box Canyon 22

    Low Water in the Box Canyon 23

Railroad Ranch (Harriman State Park) 25

    Hatches on the Ranch 27

Osborne Bridge to Riverside 29

Riverside to Warm River 32

Warm River to Ashton 37

Ashton Reservoir 39

Ashton Reservoir to St. Anthony 40

St. Anthony to the Snake River 43

Major Tributaries 45

    Buffalo River 45

    Warm River 46

    Fall River 47

    Teton River 48

Whitefish: Caught and Cussed, but Misunderstood . . 49

CHAPTER 2   Seasons of the River 52

Winter 52

Spring 55

Summer 57

Autumn 61

CHAPTER 3   Salmon Flies 63

Fishing Nymphs 66

Fishing Dry Flies 68

CHAPTER 4   Caddisflies 72
CHAPTER 5   Mayflies 81
              Blue-Winged Olive *81*
              Western March Brown *83*
              Pale Morning Dun *84*
              Trico *86*
              Western Green Drake *88*
              Brown Drake *91*
              Gray Drake *94*
              Flav *95*
              Callibaetis *97*
              Mahogany Dun *99*

CHAPTER 6   Midges 101

CHAPTER 7   Terrestrials 105
              Beetles *105*
              Ants *107*
              Grasshoppers *108*
              Crickets *111*
              Cicadas *111*

CHAPTER 8   Nymphing Methods 112

CHAPTER 9   Dry-Fly Methods 118

CHAPTER 10   Streamer Methods 121

APPENDIX 1   *Hatch Chart* *126*
APPENDIX 2   *Popular Flies for the Henry's Fork* *130*
APPENDIX 3   *Recipes for Twelve Key Flies* *134*
APPENDIX 4   *The Henry's Fork Foundation* *138*

              Suggested Reading *140*
              Index *141*
              About the Authors *148*

ILLUSTRATIONS

Lower Mesa Falls . . . . frontispiece

Map xi

Henrys' Lake 9

Henry's Lake Outlet 11

Box Canyon 18

Railroad Ranch 24

Above Hatchery Ford 32

Upper Mesa Falls 34

Chester Backwater 41

Below St. Anthony 44

Warm River 46

Winter near St. Anthony 54

Salmon Fly 58

Island Park Reservoir 61

Above Ashton 67

Weed Beds on the Railroad Ranch 78

White *Wyethia* 79

Gray Drakes 93

Below Ashton Dam 95

Rainbow with Foam Beetle 106

Henry's Fork Vista 122

Key Flies

    Black Foam Beetle 134

    Diving Blue-Winged Olive Egg Layer 134

    Emergent Sparkle Pupa – Bright Green 134

    Half Back Emerger – Blue-Winged Olive 135

    Henry's Fork Golden Stone 135

    Henry's Fork Hopper 135

    Henry's Fork Salmon Fly 136

    No-Hackle – Slate Tan 136

    Pheasant Tail Nymph 136

    Prince Nymph 137

    Rusty Hen Spinner 137

    Spent Partridge Caddis, Peacock 137

PREFACE
BY GARY LAFONTAINE

T his book started out as several hours of recorded interview between its authors—more of a conversation, really, that took advantage of two persons' combined experience on the Henry's Fork. Born and raised on the river, Mike brought to the project more than forty years experience fly fishing, guiding, and observing the river from its headwaters to its confluence with the South Fork of the Snake River.

Though not as continuously, I too have fished the Henry's Fork for twenty-plus years. I spent one fall season, 1979, on the river collecting insects at six sites once every three days for shipment to Dr. Oliver Flint at the Smithsonian Institution. Of course, I fished the river all summer with friends, including Fred Arbona, Jr., Paul Brown, Tom Young, and Mike Lawson. I was collecting the insects for my book, *Caddisflies*, for the hatch charts for the Henry's Fork, but I was also fishing hard with great anglers to learn techniques for spring creek fisheries. It was a wonderful summer.

The question and answer format of the two-day recording session, captured and presented in the acclaimed audio tape, *Fly Fishing the Henry's Fork*, is transformed and updated here into book form. It is presented in a single voice, Mike's, though, obviously, there were two voices and give and take recorded throughout the session.

There was also a third "voice" not actually heard in the audio tape—the voice calling suggestions from the other room, the voice making us go over a particular point two and three times until we got it right, and finally the voice that belonged to the hand and mind that cut and spliced the eight hours of raw tape into an easy-listening, ninety-minute format. That voice belonged to project editor Stan Bradshaw—he was our intellectual guide.

This book reads so well because it is such tight copy. The three of us: Mike, Stan, and I, created the audio version and it is because this written version started as an audio tape that it is such a fast-paced, information-packed book on the Henry's Fork.

The credit for really knowing the Henry's Fork goes to Mike. He was amazing. Often, during the taping session, I wanted to reach for pad and pencil to make notes while he was talking. Then, I would remember that I didn't have to write down his words, that everything was being recorded. Still, there were many moments when I wished that his ideas were down on paper. Now they are.

Finally, I learned about more than the Henry's Fork from Mike Lawson. I learned a lot about fly fishing. So will you. And you will enjoy reading about a great trout river.

THE HENRY'S FORK
of Idaho

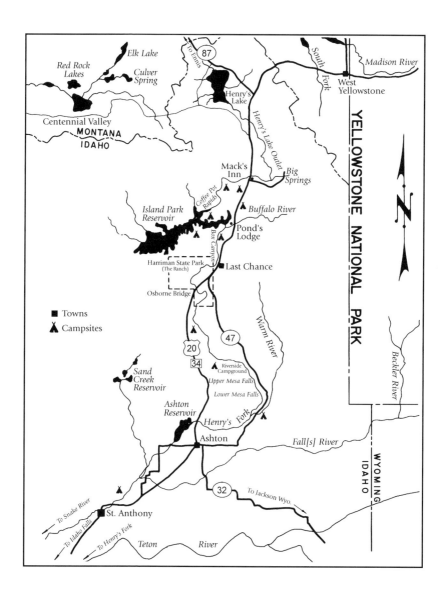

INTRODUCTION

One day many years ago in my shop, I found myself in a discussion with a bunch of experienced anglers after a frustrating day out on the river. They were in a heated argument as to which species of mayfly the trout were feeding on. The Latin was flying so thick that I felt like I was back in ancient Rome. Meanwhile there was an older fellow that came into the store to pick up a couple of flies. He was dressed like a local—old cowboy boots, a flannel shirt, and a feed supply hat. One of the experts recognized him. Earlier that day apparently he'd been out on the Ranch, really catching fish. So the guy called him over, and said, "Sir, what species of mayfly were you imitating? You were really getting the fish! Was it a *Baetis* or an *Ephemerella inermis*?" The guy stared at them with a puzzled look, thought for a minute and said, "Naw, I was just using these little gray suckers." (He didn't really say "suckers" but the word he used was real close.) That kind of experience brings us back to reality. He was just doing things right, maybe, and the other guys weren't.

A fisherman coming in to fish the Fork has certain pre-conceptions. The first of those is that he will fish the Railroad Ranch Section—world renowned for classic dry-fly fishing for big, picky fish. Of course the second preconception is that he is going to catch big fish on the Railroad Ranch Section. The big fish are there and they can be caught, but too often, the techniques that people use when they come to the Henry's Fork are not always the best ones to catch those big fish.

The Railroad Ranch Section presents problems that are unique to it, even when compared to other sections of the Henry's Fork. The Ranch section can be pretty confusing because it is such a big, wide river. There isn't a lot of definition—pockets, pools, and definite holding places. So you have to learn how to search for big fish, find big fish, and actually fish to those fish. Or if you're just going to blind cast, you have to fish an area where you're going to have a good chance to catch the larger fish.

One day I slipped away early in the morning, when the light was right, to try to photograph some trout in the lower part of the Railroad Ranch. I found a good trout feeding in a shallow cove. He wasn't rising much but I could easily see him drifting under the surface, picking off nymphs which would soon be emerging. I got some very good photos of the fish, both under the surface and rising, which I now use in one of my slide presentations.

After I had the photos I needed, I sat lazily on the bank, enjoying the morning sun. It was great watching the big fish feed. I've learned more from watching how trout feed and how they react to their environment than all of the books I've ever read.

Soon a couple of anglers walked up the trail. When they saw me they politely asked if I was fishing there. I told them I didn't mind if they fished there but before I had a chance to tell them about the big trout I had been watching, they waded in and began casting. They randomly covered the water as they waded out and upstream.

I watched the now terrorized trout race upstream until he burrowed into a weed bed where he doubtless spent the next several hours. I tipped my hat to my big, fine spotted friend. I would be back to do battle with him another day. In the meantime I reflected upon the mistakes these two anglers had made. I watched them cast and from the way the line glided in a tight loop and settled upon the water, I realized they knew how to use a fly rod. I imagined that only a few hours earlier they had stopped in the shop and picked up a selection of the appropriate fly patterns. They certainly didn't seem to lack in fly-fishing skill or knowledge. It was an understanding of the peculiar features of the Railroad Ranch Section that they lacked.

Most of the time, if you're blind fishing and you're presenting the fly well, you may not catch any 15-inch fish, but you will likely get a lot of 10- to 15-inch trout. On the other hand, even blind fishing, you still stand a chance of catching some really big fish with a big attractor. Sometimes a big Royal Wulff will pull a big monster to it. When the fish are rising, but not predictably, one way to improve your odds blind casting is to fish below a riffle.

One of the most difficult challenges of the Henry's Fork is locating big trout. I've been on some tailwater streams, like the Missouri in Montana, where I've seen dozens of big trout all podded up, feeding together. The Henry's Fork isn't like that. The bigger trout don't usually like to hang with a lot of other trout, especially smaller fish. They have certain places where they like to feed and there is often no rhyme or reason as to why. There are definitely places they like and they are in the same places year after year.

Back in my guiding days my clients used to think I had the eyes of an eagle. I would walk them into the Ranch and approach an area where I knew there were always big trout. When I was a hundred yards away I'd tell them to stop, that I had spotted a big trout sipping softly in the current. I'd give them my binoculars and sure enough, they could see a huge feeding trout. They just couldn't believe that I could see the soft dimple of a big trout over one hundred yards away. I would never reveal that I knew the trout would be there before I ever saw it. It really helps to know a river like the Henry's Fork.

It can sometimes be tough to spot the rise forms of a big fish. The big ones usually don't make a lot of disturbance in the water. One of the best ways to tell is the sound the fish makes when it rises. A big fish makes kind of a gulp. Also, look for where the fish is holding. Generally, when you see a lot of rises in one area, it will be either a group of whitefish, or a group of small to medium size trout. It may be a little bit of both. But the big trout generally will select a place to feed away from the other risers. And often they're not exactly where you think they would be holding, even though the trout prefer the deeper water when they are not feeding. When they come out to feed, sometimes they will be in water that just barely covers their backs.

Once you find a big feeding trout, you must try to get in a good position to make a drag-free presentation. The most popular approach on the Henry's Fork is to cast quartering downstream to the fish. With this approach you can feed slack line and drift the fly down over the fish. But don't make the mistake of believing the downstream drift is the only way to take trout on the Henry's Fork. There are advantages and disadvantages to every approach. You need to be able to "fish the clock" to be successful. Sometimes the best way is to get below and cast upstream to a feeding trout.

No matter how you approach, get as close to the fish as you can. The closer you are, the better your chances of a drag-free drift. Bing Lempke and Bill Goff were two of the best fishermen that I've ever seen on the Ranch. Both used similar equipment—automatic reels, a piece of equipment that had its heyday in the decades just before and after World War II. Most of the time, they would get almost right on top of a rising fish and, not making any false casts, they would accurately put the fly right over the trout's nose. When they hooked a trout, they landed him in a hurry by using a fairly heavy tippet and putting the pressure on. While it wasn't the prettiest form of fishing, it was extremely effective. Both have passed on but I still think of them often. I learned a lot about fishing from them.

The other problem with the Ranch is that if it is easy for you to see fish, then they can likely see you. You can tell if a fish is aware of you because, even if he is still rising, he'll often start moving off, ignoring your fly. When that happens, you know you've been snubbed. When that happens, stay right where you are. Don't try to follow him. If you're patient, he'll likely come back.

But these are just some of the problems on one stretch of the Henry's Fork. Each section of the river presents its own challenges, distinct from those on every other reach. So you have to prepare for the water you plan to fish.

CHAPTER 1

Sections of the River

I have spent my entire life on the Henry's Fork and have fished it from its source down to its confluence with the South Fork of the Snake River—almost one hundred miles of water. I believe it offers more diverse water than any river in the world.

Most of the attention on the Henry's Fork over the years has focused on the section below Island Park Reservoir and its dam, including Box Canyon and Harriman State Park. This section is only a fraction of the entire watershed; the Henry's Fork offers much more. While the Railroad Ranch water now offers some of the finest dry-fly fishing in the country, there are other stretches that also offer good fishing for large trout.

HENRY'S LAKE, HOME OF THE BIG BROOKIES

If you want to catch a big trout—over five pounds—go to Henry's Lake, where you have cutthroats, brook trout, and cutthroat/rainbow hybrids. This natural lake tripled in size with the building of a dam in the 1920s. Even with the dam it is still a shallow lake, with an average depth of about 18 feet and a maximum depth of about 23 feet. It has been known for its large trout since General Howard's army camped on its shore during the pursuit of Chief Joseph and the Nez Perce in 1877.

My favorite fish in Henry's Lake is the brook trout. They are not generally known to get very big, at least in most areas, but they do get to be pretty good sized in Henry's Lake. In fact, if you look at the state records for brook trout, all of the top fish came from Henry's Lake. They spawn in the fall, so the best time to get a big one is in September and October. Concentrate your fishing near the mouths of the creeks coming into the lake.

Most of the land around Henry's Lake is private. There are a couple of public access points—including the Henry's Lake State Park—where you can camp and launch your boat. There are also some good private resorts which offer camping, lodging, food, boat rental, and launch facilities. In general, you need a boat to really cover the water. The best fishing areas change as the season changes. In general the trout are scattered all over the lake early in the year. In mid-summer, when the water temperature warms, they move into the springs and to the deeper parts of the lake. With colder autumn temperatures, they again move back to the creeks and springs.

Staley Springs, on the western side of the lake, is the most popular spot to fish Henry's Lake. One reason it is so popular is because you can put in your float tube and paddle less than one hundred yards to the fishing. There is an old streambed there, and the anglers tend to concentrate around that streambed.

Almost any place on the lake where a feeder stream comes into the lake is a good place to fish. There are about ten different feeder streams that feed Henry's Lake. Use the map in this book or a good topographic map to locate these streams. You'll need a boat to get to most of them. There are several commercial places where you can rent a boat if you don't have your own.

There are also some springs that come up from the bottom of the lake. These provide some of the best fishing in the lake, but it is really tough to find them if you don't know the lake well. One way to find at least a decent spot is to watch where other boats concentrate. When somebody comes into our shop and asks where to fish Henry's Lake, I just tell them to go and fish where everybody else is fishing. I also tell them to watch how the anglers are fishing.

Henry's Lake, even more than the rest of the Henry's Fork drainage, is a really good place to hire a guide. A good guide will be able to put you on good water without a lot of searching. Besides putting you on good water, he will be able to show you, first hand, the techniques that work here. Lake flies are pretty specialized and so is the equipment. You need to have a line with the proper sink rate for the depth you fish.

If you go out on Henry's Lake and expect to catch fish on dry flies, you're going to be disappointed. Generally, you need to get under the surface for these fish. To do that, start with a type 3 sinking line to allow the fly to sink to the correct depth. If you can't get your fly to the fish, you aren't going to score. One of the biggest mistakes anglers make is to try to use a floating or sink-tip line and put some additional weight on the leader to get the fly down. The problem with that is that the floating part of the line will just keep pulling the fly back up toward the surface. A full sinking line will get the fly down and keep it down during the retrieve.

To successfully fish deep, you have to address three main things: lake depth, fly pattern, and method of retrieve.

Float-tubing anglers on Henry's Lake may have a chance at good-sized brook trout, especially in the fall. (Photo by Janet and Marty Downey)

To find the proper depth, use the countdown method with the sinking line. Make a cast and wait a few seconds, counting before you start to retrieve. If you don't get a strike or touch the weeds or other bottom structure, your fly probably isn't getting deep enough. Make another cast and count longer before you start to retrieve to allow the line to sink deeper. Stay with this method until you drag the bottom or get a strike.

One of the most common misconceptions is to think that if you aren't catching trout, you don't have the right fly. Bill Schiess is one of the best anglers on Henry's Lake. You're likely to find him out on the lake any day except Sunday, when he goes to church. He always carries several different fly lines of varying sink rates. He is also a master at varying his retrieve. He has some killer fly patterns, but having the right fly isn't the only thing that makes Bill successful. Varying the retrieve and keeping the fly in the zone is equally important. Bill's book, *Fishing Henry's Lake*, describes his fly patterns and has excellent maps which show the top fishing areas at different times of the season.

A really effective technique on Henry's Lake is the yo-yo method. Use the fastest sinking line you can find and let it go right to the bottom, with a buoyant fly on the end of the tippet. I like to use a foam-bodied fly and tie on a smaller wet pattern as a dropper. The foam fly doesn't sink, and so it doesn't get into the weeds. On the retrieve, every pull on the line makes the fly dart downward. With this method, you can move the fly across weedy flats without snagging too many weeds. And the trout seem to like it. When the fishing is slow, this method will attract strikes when standard retrieves won't.

Three LaFontaine patterns, the Floating Damsel, Floating Emergent Sparkle Pupa, and Floating Marabou Single Egg, with their built-in foam, are specifically tied for the yo-yo method. Using two Marabou Single Eggs, and retrieving them slowly off the creek mouths is deadly for brook trout in the fall.

As for more traditional fly patterns, mohair and rabbit fur leeches, Woolly Worms in browns, greens and olives, shrimp patterns in olive and gray, damselfly nymphs, and a variety of Woolly Buggers and Krystal Buggers are some of the most popular types of flies for the lake.

HENRY'S LAKE OUTLET

Above its confluence with the main stem of the Henry's Fork, the outlet from Henry's Lake is a small stream, comfortable to fish. If you get up close to the Henry's Lake Dam, though, it can really be a fiasco. There are usually a very high number of big cutthroats and hybrids which move down through the dam where they try to spawn. Early in the season, the outlet really gets heavy fishing pressure. There are

Above its confluence with the main stem of the Henry's Fork, the outlet from Henry's Lake is a small, comfortable-to-fish stream. (Photo by Mike Lawson)

some pretty nice fish in this stretch. It isn't what I'd call real quality fishing; it's more of a meat hole where anything goes. There are no special regulations, so you'll see a lot of bait slingers who will likely be trying to fill their limit of two cutthroat trout.

If you go downstream a short distance, you can get away from the crowds. You probably won't catch as many fish, but you can still have some really good small stream fishing without so much company. My favorite area is the section which flows through the Flat Ranch just below the Highway 20 bridge. This reach of the river used to be hammered by grazing. But the Nature Conservancy acquired and now manages the Flat Ranch. The Nature Conservancy has worked hard to restore the magnificent grasslands, wetlands, and other wildlife habitat. The ranch is also a management demonstration project where cattle ranchers and wildlife enthusiasts work together toward a common goal. This part of the stream has made a tremendous comeback from its former degraded state. With better managed stream flows the future is bright for quality fishing throughout the season. Spend some time at the Flat Ranch visitor's center to get a good understanding of the Nature Conservancy's program for the ranch.

COFFEE POT AREA

Big Springs is about a mile above the confluence of the Henry's Lake Outlet. Here the entire Henry's Fork boils out of underground springs at about 200 cubic feet per second, or 480,000 gallons a day at a constant 52 degrees Fahrenheit. All of that clean, clear water pouring right out of the ground is a sight worth seeing.

The fishing is closed from here to Henry's Lake Outlet, and there are always a bunch of lazy, huge trout hanging out at the bridge where they long have been a major tourist attraction in Island Park. People like to feed them. At least if the river beats you up, you can go to Big Springs and see some huge rainbows.

An old friend, Cecil Brown, was a game warden in Island Park in the early seventies. He told me he once got a call about a poacher at Big Springs so he drove up to check it out. When he arrived there was a fly fisherman waded in just below the bridge where a large crowd had gathered. He was decked out from top to bottom with the finest fly-fishing attire and gear of the day. Every time he hooked a trout, the crowd cheered. He carefully released each trout brought to net. When the warden reminded him he was fishing illegally and that he would be issued a citation, he replied, "I've been fishing for the past two weeks, hiring the top guides around. When I add up how much money I've spent and averaged it out, I've spent several hundred dollars a fish. Just let me know how much this costs and I'll be happy to pay. This is the best fishing of my life!"

Of course I asked Cecil how much it cost the guy. He didn't think it was too much because he hadn't killed any trout and the only thing he could cite the guy for was fishing in closed waters. Maybe that guy had us all fooled.

Highway 20 crosses the Henry's Fork at Mack's Inn, about two miles below Big Springs. From here the river picks up speed as it narrows through the Coffee Pot Rapids. This stretch is one of my favorites. You seldom meet serious fly anglers there. Although you're probably not going to catch large trout, it's a gorgeous stretch of river. But it is truly rapid. You don't want to take a boat down here because you probably won't make it.

You get a lot of fish from 10 inches to about 13 or 14 inches. Early in the season and later in autumn, you have a good chance of tagging a real big trout up from the Island Park Reservoir.

During those early and late periods, to increase my chances for bigger fish, I'll use streamers and nymphs. For one thing, I'm not fishing at a time of year when there's much activity on the surface, so generally, I have three logical choices: streamers, nymphs, and egg patterns. The egg patterns are really successful in the fall because this part of the river gets a good run of Kokanee Salmon, which are landlocked sockeye salmon. The Kokanee average between about 15 and 17 inches long. And they spawn in the upper reaches of the river. You get a situation like you might find in Alaska, with rainbows moving along with these salmon to feed on their spawn. Flesh Flies also work in October and November, after the salmon die, because big trout also feed on their carcasses.

Once the insects do start to move, the Coffee Pot stretch gets some great hatches. The Salmon Flies are prolific in the fast water. Both the Green Drakes and the Brown Drakes emerge heavily in quieter sections above. And if the crowds down on the Ranch get to you during the Green Drake hatch, Coffee Pot Rapids can be a good place to fish in some solitude and still get into good Green Drake action.

The Coffee Pot Campground is located below Mack's Inn, about a mile above the rapids. It is gentle, quiet water. The campground is beautiful and the fishing is well suited for a family outing. I can't think of a better place to get a youngster into some small trout with a fly rod.

Island Park Reservoir

Island Park Reservoir is a large, shallow reservoir. It isn't as well known for fly fishing as Henry's Lake or Hebgen Lake. It's a little more inconsistent than those lakes. You can go out one day and find fish rising all over the place, and go back the same time the next day with the same conditions and find hardly a trout rising at all. But it is worth going back and back and back because the reservoir has really big fish. I have seen rainbows in the six- to seven-pound range rising for small dry flies. We have had several guide clients land fish that weighed in double digits.

Island Park Reservoir has a good food chain which enables the trout to grow fast and large. It has a rich zooplankton base and lots of mayflies, shrimp, damselflies, leeches, and small forage fish. This diversity creates a healthy food chain.

The most common forage fish is the Utah Chub. These fish are prolific and they quickly get large enough to eat a well-placed worm from a bait fisherman. Luckily they seldom hit flies. In the past the Idaho Department of Fish and Game (IDFG) battled the chub population by periodically killing the lake with rotenone. They have done this at least three times since 1959. It was a waste of time because the chubs always come back. In the meantime, the entire food chain is lost and the fishing in the lake takes years to recover.

The last time was in 1992. It appears the state has finally learned a hard lesson because IDFG has stated that it will never do it again.

The large population of forage fish gives rise to a unique feeding behavior called "busting fry." You'll see a big commotion in the shallows when large fish, often several of them, herd schools of small fish, pass through them and hit them hard. Once the big fish have charged into a school of small fish it will make a swing back through them, and often there will be an injured fish right on the surface, wriggling around. When you find this, tie on a floating injured minnow pattern, cast it out into the general area, twitch it slightly, and then hang on. This same technique works really well on the river, too.

There are also some impressive aquatic insect hatches on the reservoir—especially mayflies and midges. The primary species of mayfly is the *Callibaetis*—a speckled-wing mayfly. The fish usually key on the spinner. It comes onto the lake in the morning hours, all the way from early July into early October in some years. The duns seem to emerge very sporadically, but I've learned that a cripple, fished in the surface film, is often more effective than a spent spinner. This is because the trout cruise just under the surface, making their window of vision quite small. They don't see insects that are sitting on top of the water until they are right under them. A cripple, on the other hand, protrudes through the surface film and a trout can see it from several feet away. You can also give your fly a slight twitch to help the trout spot it.

A size-14 Shroud, a heavily hackled gray dry fly with a red marabou tail, is the perfect cripple pattern. The front half rides high—great for twitching—and scores incredible catches during *Callibaetis* time on Island Park.

Another tactic for cruising trout that are feeding on *Callibaetis* is to use a nymph with a greased leader. I use a slender-bodied pattern with ostrich herl for gills in size 14. Cast a few feet ahead of a cruiser, wait until he approaches, and then twitch the nymph with a slow retrieve. The trout will often charge and bust the nymph hard.

The late-morning arrival of *Callibaetis* can pose a problem for the angler on the reservoir, because the wind often comes up about the same time. It can be tough to work a dry fly in those reservoir winds, but sometimes you can be successful with a long rod, light line (three-weight), 16-foot leader, and heavily hackled dry fly. Then go *with* the wind, don't fight it. This is not true "dapping," but it is a compromise method with tackle most anglers carry and lets you fish on windy days. Find the flat ribbons of water, known as scum lines, in the chop.

Because of the wind, you are often better off to use the same techniques described for Henry's Lake: A sinking line and variable retrieve. On the reservoir, however, you may want to use a faster sinking line, because you'll sometimes be covering deeper water.

Fluctuations in the reservoir level can have a big influence on the fishing. In the spring, when it's high, the water spreads over large flats and you get a lot more cruising fish working the weed beds. In the summer, when it's drawn down, the fish concentrate more in the central pool.

The drought years of the late 1980s and early 1990s resulted in the reservoir being drawn down to critical levels. This resulted in low stream flows below the Island Park Dam in the Box Canyon. The reservoir also was affected by extremely low water levels in the autumn and early winter, which concentrated the trout and destroyed parts of the food chain. When the lake stays full for several years, the result is an explosion of fat, large healthy rainbows.

The large reservoir flats can provide some of the most exciting fishing that you will find anywhere in the Henry's

Fork drainage. It can be just like bone fishing; the fish will be out in little channels, just working along next to the grass. And sometimes, you can even see the fish cruising in the shallow water. This is best when the damselflies start to emerge in late June and early July. The nymphs swim to the exposed weed beds where they crawl out to emerge. The trout load up on these emerging damselfly nymphs. The soft, newly hatched insects are gray. The best tactic is to use a size-10 or -12 damsel nymph and fish it in the channels between the weed beds with a floating or slow sinking fly line. I have also had some great fun casting a dry damsel pattern and twitching it across the channels. It often results in some explosive rises and bone jarring strikes.

The Island Park Reservoir has ample public access. Take the Green Canyon Road from U.S. Highway 20 past the Harriman State Park headquarters to the West End Campground. This is a Forest Service campground with a good boat ramp. You can also reach the lake from dozens of fingers west of the campground. The trout will move into the coves between the long fingers or hold just off the points. This offers great opportunities and easy access for float tubes and pontoon boats.

Box Canyon

Below Island Park Reservoir, the river flows through the dam into the Box Canyon, the first really famous stretch of the river. This section stretches about three miles down to the mouth of the canyon where the water flattens out. The Box Canyon is fast, rough, shallow water moving through big, angular boulders. This stretch can be tough to wade. You don't have the rounded rocks that you would see in the Madison. And that's what makes it so difficult to wade; each step lands on something unexpected.

Box Canyon stretches for three miles of fast, rough, shallow water running through big boulders that make wading difficult. (Photo by Glenda Bradshaw)

This is serious big-fish water. It is full of food, and it has the other ingredient for big fish—a lot of wonderful holding water.

While there are a variety of insects in the Box Canyon, the only insects that seem to really entice many of the larger fish to the surface are the big flies: the Salmon Flies and the slightly smaller Golden Stones. With big chunks of food available near the bottom, the big fish don't seem to waste their energy coming to the surface for small insects.

Maturing populations of caddisfly larvae, mayfly nymphs, and several species of stonefly nymphs produce trout food on a seasonal basis. Large Salmon Fly nymphs that take up to four years to mature provide year-round nutrition for the trout to grow large and fat. A huge population of leeches, crayfish, sculpins, and other forage fish supplement the insect diet.

Without the Salmon Fly, I don't think we'd find nearly as many big fish as we do. In fact, you can work a big stonefly nymph through here at any time of the season and have a good chance of moving fish. If I was to pick only one fly to use in the Box Canyon, it would probably be a size-4 or -6 black chenille Rubber Legs Nymph to imitate the stonefly. It should be heavily weighted so you can bounce it right down in the rocks.

Streamers are also effective in the Box. I like Woolhead Sculpins, with rabbit fur bodies and rabbit strip tails. Zonkers and Conehead Buggers are also effective patterns. In the early morning and late evening hours the big trout move into the shallows. You can usually move trout with a floating line in slow water. In the fast water a short sink-tip and a weighted fly will get the fly down quickly.

The Island Park Dam has been both a blessing and a curse to the Box Canyon. The dam was built in the 1930s and the Island Park Reservoir has been stocked heavily with hatchery trout ever since. During low water years these trout were flushed through the dam into the river below. Studies funded by the Henry's Fork Foundation have indicated that the one reason trout populations have fluctuated so much in the Box Canyon is because of the periodic, inadvertent stocking of hatchery trout from the Island Park Reservoir.

The wild trout population is limited because the dam also stopped the upstream migration of trout to their traditional spawning grounds. The Buffalo River, a large spring-fed tributary, enters the Box Canyon a few hundred yards below the dam. It also is blocked by a hydro dam that prevents trout from using it for spawning and overwintering habitat. The Henry's Fork Foundation has cooperated with the dam operator to install a fish ladder to enable the Box Canyon trout to utilize the Buffalo River.

In 1992 Fall River Electric Cooperative retro-fit a hydro facility into the Island Park Dam. The Federal Energy

Regulatory Commission (FERC) license conditions require water quality standards which are much better than the natural flow of the river. The water temperature, turbidity, and dissolved oxygen are now controlled at the dam for the benefit of the fishery. In this way, the hydro facility actually provides a benefit to the Box Canyon fishery.

On the other hand, with the modifications to the dam operation, we may never again see the numbers of giant trout which once populated the Box Canyon because most of them probably came down through the dam from the reservoir above.

(A friend of mine once caught a rainbow that was 18½ pounds on a floating Rapala in this stretch. I've never found a fly to match a Rapala, and boy, are those Rapalas tough to cast with a fly rod.)

The outflow of the reservoir is now screened to prevent fish passage. The Box Canyon is now a self-sustaining, wild trout fishery without hatchery trout support from Island Park Reservoir. I don't know if that matters to you, but it does to me. There is something special about the connection between an angler and a wild trout. I am in awe of a 20-inch wild trout. To know that it was spawned in the river, battled through the threats of predators and hazards of the river, and survived the fight for its life is an important part of my fishing. For this reason, I think the future for the Box Canyon is better than the past.

Despite its rough water, the Box Canyon fishes well either wading or from a boat. I recommend fishing from a boat when fishing streamers. It's fun to float the canyon really early in the morning, just at daylight, and cast a sculpin pattern right into the bank in the shallow water, and see the fish come out for it. If you're going to move those fish off the banks, you have to do it at daylight or just at dark.

STONEFLIES IN THE BOX CANYON

Usually, the Salmon Fly emergence in the Box Canyon will take place during the first or second week of June—typically June 5 through June 10. This can vary a lot, however. If you were to come out for five straight years, trying to hit the dry-fly fishing during the Salmon Fly hatch, you would probably average hitting it one out of those five years. But I've caught my biggest fish in Box Canyon on dry Salmon Fly patterns.

If you really want to catch fish on dry flies in the Canyon, however, don't come during the Salmon Fly hatch. Come when the Golden Stones are on. The Golden Stone hatches begin the last week of June, about the time the Green Drakes start hatching in the Railroad Ranch section. The good thing about the Golden Stone hatch is that it will continue until the first part of August.

You need three dry stonefly styles to cover the Salmon Flies and Golden Stones. High-floating patterns, such as a Fluttering Stone, that can be skittered and fluttered on the surface are important. Impart action to the fly to mimic the commotion these big flies make when they first hit the water. High-visibility patterns, like an Improved Sofa Pillow, which float low but are still easy to see are great for fishing the fast, rough water. You also need low profile floaters, such as a Bird's Stonefly, which give the appearance of a stonefly resting on the surface in the quieter sections.

Fishing stoneflies in the Box Canyon can be different than other rivers because there are usually more trout holding in the middle of the river than along the banks. The fish will come boiling out on the surface in the fastest water to slam an adult stone. That's why you really need to be patient and cover the water carefully. Just because you follow another angler through a run doesn't necessarily lessen your chances at a big trout.

HIGH WATER IN THE BOX CANYON

The highest releases from the Island Park Dam usually occur in midsummer when the irrigation demand is highest. Higher flows can be intimidating because they make the river much more difficult to wade. But there are some definite advantages to higher flows, because they disperse the trout and the larger fish like to move in along the banks. Fishing from a drift boat can be most efficient because you can cover more water. During high water, use streamer patterns. Higher flows move the big fish out of the deepest holding water and into shallow water, making them more vulnerable to a well presented streamer pattern.

Big nymphs can also be really effective during high water. The most popular method is to use an indicator with a heavily weighted nymph. I personally don't like using indicators. I grew up fishing the Box Canyon with weighted nymphs using the "high stick" method. Keep a short line and cast upstream into the current. As the line drifts down you lift the tip of the rod high to keep the slack out of the line as you track the nymph downstream with the tip of your rod. As the fly drifts below you need to lower the rod tip to allow a longer drift. At the end of the drift the nymph will rise to the surface because of the tension on the line. The strike can occur at any time so you need to keep an eye on the tip of the line for the slightest hesitation. The greatest advantage of the high stick technique is you can keep the nymph deep by lowering the rod tip when it drifts into a deeper slot. You lose this advantage when you use an indicator because it keeps the nymph at the same level.

Nonetheless, a strike indicator offers a distinct advantage when you are fishing a nymph from a drift boat. An indicator actually does three things: (1) It indicates how the nymph is drifting. If you have drag on the indicator you can be assured that the nymph is also drifting unnaturally. (2) It indicates the strike. If it pops down or hesitates, you should set the hook. (3) It keeps the fly at the same level. This may be the most important function of all. In fact if we all weren't purists (i.e. snobby fly fishermen) we'd probably just call it what it is—a bobber.

There are many different kinds of indicators. The hard poly-foam indicators are probably the most popular. I prefer bright buoyant yarn. There are plenty of good commercial yarn indicators but you can buy a skein of polypropylene macramé yarn and you're set for life. It is important to adjust the indicator to the proper distance on the leader from the fly. A good rule is one and one half times the depth of the water to compensate for the current.

Most of the guides tie a big fluff ball of yarn at the end of the butt section below the tip of the fly line. They then tie a long section of 2X tippet material directly above the yarn with an improved clinch knot. The fly is then tied about five or six feet below the yarn, depending on the depth of the water.

LOW WATER IN THE BOX CANYON

The stream flows are reduced as the demand for irrigation diminishes later in the season. By mid-September the flow is normally about half as much as it is in July. This offers the advantage of being able to wade many spots which would be impossible in midsummer. There are some disadvantages, however. The bigger trout become much more skittish with lower water.

You need to modify your technique if you expect to catch large trout in low water conditions. First change your fly patterns. Stonefly nymphs are still productive but instead of using a size 4 or 6, drop down to a size 10 or 12. Small beadhead nymphs are also very productive. My favorite is a size-16 or -18 Beadhead Pheasant Tail. Sometimes I use a tandem rig with a small Prince Nymph as the top fly and a smaller nymph as a dropper about 12 inches below.

Through the Railroad Ranch section the Henry's Fork widens into a wide, shallow spring creek that anglers often call the Bonefish Flats. (Photo by Mike Lawson)

Drop down a couple of sizes on the diameter of the leader tippet. Wade more carefully and try to not grind the rocks any more than necessary. Aluminum stream cleats and a wading staff are a definite advantage, but they also make enough noise from grinding against the rocks to send trout running for cover fifty feet away.

The catch rate for larger trout normally diminishes with lower water. Boats must float right through the best holding water to get through the shallows. With trout concentrated in the deeper water, a boat can spook the entire pool. Our guides frequently walk the boat so they can keep away from the best runs and not disturb the fish.

When the water is low it is best to wait for bad weather. It seems like the trout are more confident when the weather is nasty and dark. Dress warm and wear good fingerless gloves. You have to be willing to go out there when the weather is tough. I have caught lots of large fish when it was cold, miserable, and uncomfortable in October and November.

RAILROAD RANCH

When I refer to the Ranch, I mean what was once known as the Railroad Ranch—now known as the Harriman State Park. It is a classic spring creek in every sense, one hundred yards wide and usually not more than three feet in depth with soft flowing currents, abundant hatches of aquatic insects, and huge trout. What sets this water apart from other areas is that the trout continue to feed on small insects on the surface until they reach gigantic proportions. While they will snap up a free swimming leech or forage fish in a second, there is so much aquatic vegetation that these kinds of critters have plenty of cover from foraging trout.

The Ranch has a rich legacy and tradition. The Harriman State Park now consists of almost 10,000 acres, a combination of Forest Service land and 4,500 acres deeded to the state of Idaho from Roland and Averill Harriman. The original property was purchased by their father, E. H. Harriman. Although he never saw the Ranch, his sons came to love and enjoy it. The property was officially given to the state of Idaho to be held as a sanctuary for wildlife and their environment. The Harriman brothers insisted on strong, permanent covenants to ensure the property would be protected for generations.

Roland was a fly fisher. The seven miles of river which flow through the Ranch were designated as "fly fishing only" long before it became a fashionable management tool in other areas. Charles Brooks wrote in his great book, *The Henry's Fork*, that Roland truly lived up to an injunction he said he received from his father, "whatever you touch, leave it better for your having touched it." From time to time anglers who share his love for the Ranch have defended it tenaciously whenever attempts have been made to try to commercialize this magnificent gift from the Harrimans.

Most of the time you have to be really committed to match the hatch. You'll almost always find a good hatch of aquatic insects, no matter what time of the season. Occasionally, however, I will use attractor patterns. One of my favorites is a Royal Wulff. I like it because I can see it, and therefore, it is easier for me to get a natural drift. Of course, it is especially good when the Royal Wulff hatch is on the water. In fact one of my favorite nymph patterns is a Prince Nymph. Whenever somebody asks me what it imitates, I always tell them, "It's the nymphal form of the Royal Wulff."

In all seriousness, when the tiniest of the tiny flies are out, the Royal Wulff can be quite effective. If you get a hatch of size-22 mayflies, and you have maybe three dozen of these naturals per square foot of water surface, how many of the naturals is the fish actually going to let drift over before he takes one? It's going to be awhile. And if you're matching the hatch exactly and getting the proper drift, you're not going to be able to tell what is your fly and, probably, neither is the fish. You need to get in a rhythm to coincide with the feeding rhythm of the trout. Take time to observe the trout's feeding pattern before you lay a bunch of casts over him and alert him to your presence. Then, if you have a little size-18 Royal Wulff on your tippet, you can time your cast so the fly arrives at the trout about when he is going to rise. It gives the fish an opportunity to see something a little different, and the trout will sometimes take the odd fly. It is important to use a small Wulff, however. More often than not, size is much more important than pattern. A couple of other great patterns for "breaking the hatch" are a Renegade and a Black Beetle.

Is this "Wild Thing" theory a guaranteed method? Not hardly. It is something to try when you are frustrated, and it will remind you of the importance of good presentation. Hatches should not be intimidating.

HATCHES ON THE RANCH

The traditional opening day for the Harriman Ranch Section is June 15. Before June 15, hatches concentrate at Last Chance, just north of the Ranch boundary. By the time the Ranch opens for fishing, the hatches are in full swing with several caddisfly and mayfly species.

Some kind of hatching will generally go on throughout most of the day, unless the weather is too hot. Mornings— early mornings—usually see spinners on the water. The duns—Pale Morning Duns and Green Drakes—come off in midmorning; then in the evenings you get most of the cad- dis activity. There is usually a heavy spinner fall just at dusk. Down in the slow water, around the Railroad Ranch build- ings and below the Osborne Bridge, at Wood Road #16, you see the Brown Drakes.

In midseason, from mid-July through August, you can get good concentrated hatches. Often the fishing will be more difficult. During midsummer, when the water is higher from increased releases from Island Park Dam, concentrate on the bank sippers. That's when the trout move in along the banks where they can pick up food that concentrates there. The mid-river fishing gets harder because it is difficult to get a good drag-free drift with the undulating currents flowing over the aquatic vegetation.

During any time of the year, one particular weather condition will provide a better opportunity than any other. The ideal hatch conditions will occur when it's not very warm—maybe in the sixties—and humid with a good cloud cover. A slight drizzle, with no wind makes for per- fect conditions.

Conversely, some of the worse hatch conditions occur when it is really hot and dry, with maybe a little bit of a breeze to even make it drier. In those conditions, the insects just don't survive when they hatch. During a hot spell, about the only thing you can do, if you're really dedicated to using the dry fly, is get up early in the morning and be out there at dawn or wait until later in the evening.

Windy conditions are not all bad, however. When there are duns hatching and when there's a mayfly hatch in progress, the wind usually doesn't stop that hatch from coming off, but it becomes very difficult to find rising fish. It is hard to see them because they will just poke their noses up, making small rises forms obscured by the riffle on the water. But if you can find rising fish, it is a lot easier to fish to them. The riffled surface will mask the disturbance of your line and leader on the water. You can also get closer to a trout, sometimes almost right on top of it. The prevailing wind direction also works to your advantage. The prevailing wind is from the south, blowing upstream. This upstream wind makes it easier to slip in just below a feeding trout.

At times, crowds on the Ranch can be heavy enough to make you want to go somewhere else. We see the biggest crowds from June 15 when the Ranch opens until July 4. While it has become difficult to totally avoid the crowds on the Ranch, if you don't mind walking down into Harriman State Park a mile or so, generally you can find water that is not crowded with a lot of other fishermen.

The Green Drake hatch is the primary cause of the big crowds. It comes off in the middle part of the morning, so that's when the Ranch will be elbow to elbow. But you can find a lot of areas to yourself if you wait until afternoon. And in the evenings in late June, there are great hatches, especially caddisflies, and the crowds won't be as bad.

If you plan to travel specifically to fish the Ranch, consider waiting until August and September. There are some really good hatches then and they normally last throughout the day. The natural insects are smaller, which intimidates many anglers, who will go elsewhere in pursuit of easier prey. I love August and September and I spend as much of my free time as possible fishing the Ranch.

OSBORNE BRIDGE TO RIVERSIDE

The water from Osborne Bridge down to the Pinehaven summer home area offers another 2½ miles of prime dry-fly water which is not much different than what you find in the Railroad Ranch above. In fact, Harriman State Park also encompasses this section of the Henry's Fork. There is a deep channel, however, which runs all the way down to Pinehaven, making it virtually impossible to wade across this reach unless you are an NBA center. It is quite comical to watch an unknowing angler keep trying over and over to wade the river at different locations. The question is not whether he will make it across, but when the water will eventually pour over his waders and send him scampering to his car.

I learned this lesson many years ago when goose hunting. The air temperature was slightly above zero and I was convinced that if I could just wade across, I could get set up in the flight pattern of the geese. After several attempts at tiptoeing up to my arm pits, the water came gushing in and quickly ended my hunting trip.

Another feature of this reach is water temperature scrambled by dozens of springs. Some of them come in along the banks, including the great Osborne Spring, while others seep up through the streambed. The effect is most noticeable during the hottest time of the year, when the springs provide an infusion of cooler water into the river. You can usually feel a distinct temperature difference as you wade out into the stream.

The fish will move into the cooler water, especially if water temperatures in the main river get up over 65 degrees Fahrenheit. In places along the east bank, you can see the springs dumping into the river. The colder temperatures also significantly change the insect activity. Early in the season the springs make the main river in this section a little warmer than the rest of the river, so you get hatches sooner. Later in the season, some of the hatches will continue weeks after they have finished in the other stretches of the river. In fact the Pale Morning Duns hatch from early June until October.

The maximum size of the fish may be even a little bigger in this stretch than they are in the Ranch. There are two reasons for this. First, deeper water in the main channel offers more protection from predators and provides better overwintering habitat. Second, the dozens of springs create a more consistent temperature regime which not only produces more prolific aquatic insect populations, but also raises the metabolism of the trout. This provides an opportunity for them to stay more active throughout the entire season. It doesn't take a rocket scientist to know that a trout which feeds heavily on a plentiful food source during the winter months will grow faster and larger than a fish that has to hole up all winter because of cold water temperatures. In fact, I only know one rocket scientist who knows anything about fly fishing.

There is no question that the most selective trout in the world live about a mile below the Osborne Bridge near the Wood Road #16 access. This is where the hottest shots of the angling world concentrate to test their skills. The trout are big, fat, and extremely powerful. If you are lucky enough to hook one, you better dig in for a strong battle.

During my college years I worked as the chief of a Forest Service survey crew. We lived in a camp way back in the bush where it was impractical to drive a four-wheel vehicle in and out to go fishing. I had a powerful dirt bike that I jumped on every day as soon as work ended. The bike always took me straight to Wood Road #16.

There was an old wrecked car body that protruded just out from the bank. (It is still there but it has moved a few hundred yards downstream.) I wasted almost all of my fishing time casting to a very large trout that fed just upstream from the old car body. In my estimation, I probably cast to that fish for forty to fifty hours without even getting a decent refusal. In fact, that trout is the reason I eventually learned to tie the No-Hackle, first developed by Doug Swisher and Carl Richards in their definitive book, *Selective Trout*. I went through several dozen mallard wings before I came up with a couple of flies which looked presentable.

It was either just blind luck or I finally came up with the right pattern with the right presentation at just the right time. The big trout came up and softly sipped the fly. I just couldn't believe it! I didn't even set the hook and he actually kept rising. I lifted the rod to make another cast and he was on. He slugged it out for a couple of minutes, acting quite bored, and then he got serious. He took off for the middle of the stream gaining speed as he went. After a couple of magnificent jumps and forty yards of backing he was gone. It was like a first sexual encounter; all of the anticipation, excitement, and effort and it was over in just a few seconds. I'll never forget it. I frequently sit a few moments at the site of the old car body and reminisce. With the Henry's Fork, it isn't always the fish you catch that create the best the memories; it's often the battles you lose.

The easiest access into this area is to walk down the river from the Osborne Bridge. There are also some points of access from the east side of the river. There is an old gravel pit that is a good place to park and walk down the river. If you have a good four-wheel-drive vehicle (or a rental car) you can drive in Wood Road #16, which is rough and nasty, especially after a good rain. On the west side of the river is the Pinehaven summer home area. This is all private land, so you might get into a landowner confrontation if you drive in and try to get on the river.

Above Hatchery Ford you can hike in or, if you have an expert on the oars, float-fish some fast, rocky water. (Photo by Mike Lawson)

The character of the river in this reach is mostly flat water like on the Ranch, until you get down to the Henry's Fork Lodge, about a mile above Riverside Campground. In this next stretch, as you start getting back into the forest, the river starts to speed up again. The fishing isn't as good between the lodge and Riverside Campground. There just isn't much good holding water until you get just above the campground.

RIVERSIDE TO WARM RIVER

Most anglers never see the Henry's Fork below Riverside Campground. Yet this stretch of the river is some of the most beautiful water found in the entire Yellowstone area. It is as different from the Ranch section as night from day. It's even rougher in some areas than the Box Canyon. It's really fast water.

As a practical matter, the float-fishing opportunities are limited below Riverside until you get below Lower Mesa

Falls. And the river is tough to get into even for bank and wade fishing. The highway doesn't run right along the river. It's usually at least a mile away, but there are several old wood roads that lead in from the highway. But even when you get there, you still have to hike down into the canyon, which is a fairly decent walk. But, it can really be worth it.

I spent a lot of time in this part of the river when I was a teenager. That was when I didn't notice how steep it was to climb out of the deep canyon after a hard day's fishing. You can enter the river from the west side by roads going into Hatchery Ford and Sheep Falls. These roads can get you lost, however, because they split into several forks. Pick up a road map of the Targhee Forest at the ranger station near Pond's Lodge to minimize the time you spend aimlessly driving around.

There are more routes into the canyon stretch from the Mesa Falls scenic loop on the east side of the river between Osborne Bridge and Warm River. There is a good access road at Hatchery Ford where you can actually drive right down to the river. There is a good boat ramp there that should only be used to take out. If you put in there, you'll plunge over Mesa Falls which is more than one hundred feet high.

There is also good walk-in access at Wood Road #6 that puts you right at the edge of the canyon. From there you'll have to hike down the trail; even worse, you'll need to hike back out. There is also hike-in access at Mesa Falls and at the old ski resort at Bear Gulch. The river flows out of the canyon just above where another major tributary, Warm River, flows out of its canyon. A smaller stream, Robinson Creek, joins Warm River just above the confluence with the Henry's Fork. Both offer great small stream opportunities.

The float from Riverside to Hatchery Ford is worthwhile. There is some serious white water in this section and you shouldn't float this stretch unless you have a lot of experience

Fishing opportunities are limited to hike-in only in the stretch between Upper Mesa Falls (above) and Lower Mesa Falls. (Photo by Mike Lawson) with a raft or drift boat. There isn't a year goes by without somebody dumping a boat, and a few people have drowned. This is a good part of the river to fish when the Salmon Fly hatch is out, early in the year. The water goes so fast and there are so many rocks that it is tough to fish nymphs or streamers from a boat. You can really have some great fun with a dry fly when the trout blow up out of a pocket behind a rock.

During midsummer, the hatches tend to taper off. There are lots of places to pull over and wade fish with nymphs or streamers. During late summer you can have some good days fishing hoppers and large foam-bodied attractor patterns.

Below Hatchery Ford the river is totally inaccessible for float fishing. Two major waterfalls, Upper and Lower Mesa, and several smaller ones, including Sheep Falls, make it impossible to navigate. If you're into adventure, you can slide a boat or raft down the hill at the Grandview Campground just below Lower Mesa Falls. From there it is a very nice float down to the confluence of Warm River. There is one extremely nasty rapid section called Surprise Falls, but you can get through if you are experienced at the oars. There have been a few boats dumped there, however, and a couple of people have died, so don't even consider this float unless you are an expert white-water rower. You can't portage around the falls because of the rocks.

Sliding the boat down the mountain is also long and treacherous. Also, the trail is getting rougher by the year, causing erosion into the river. I don't think it will be many years before the Forest Service closes off this access.

One day a couple of guys came into our shop and asked my wife, Sheralee, what she knew about floating down below Lower Mesa Falls. She told them she had never done it herself but she knew it was a long, steep trail down to the river. She told them to make sure to check it out carefully before they started to slide their boat down.

They told her it was too late for that. They had been told that it wasn't a bad trail so they decided to slide their drift boat down without checking the trail out first. About half way down their boat got away and they lost it. It went sailing down the steep grade, picking up momentum as it went. There was another party at the bottom getting ready to launch a raft. They heard the noise above and saw the drift boat coming straight at them. They barely dove to safety before the drift boat hit the raft dead center. The drift boat popped the raft and then hit a big flat rock which catapulted it out into the river. It rolled over on its side and sunk. Amazingly, nobody got hurt and they even salvaged the drift boat enough to row it out.

You really need to know what you are doing when you plan this trip. It is really rough on drift boats, but it can be worth it. Take lots of strong rope to help lower the boat to the bottom. Several commercial outfitters who make this trip use pontoon rafts that are much easier than drift boats to slide down the canyon and negotiate through white water.

Below Lower Mesa Falls you get into brown trout for the first time on the Henry's Fork. In the late seventies the Idaho Fish and Game Department, with assistance from the local chapter of Trout Unlimited, stocked fingerling brown trout. These browns have really taken off in the years since. Today the Henry's Fork produces some excellent opportunities to catch large brown trout between Lower Mesa Falls and the confluence with the South Fork of the Snake.

You may need to shift in this reach from rainbow-targeted techniques to brown trout tactics. The browns seem to like to hold in the deeper, quieter pools. You'll also have a better chance to hook large browns on a streamer with a fast sinking line.

A few years ago I took Gil and Arlene Bacon on a float below Warm River. They had allowed me to hunt wild turkeys on their farm in Nebraska, and I wanted take them on a float trip to show my appreciation. We pulled in along the edge of a deep pool where Arlene hooked a nice whitefish. When she had it almost to the boat a long dark shape followed it toward the surface. It was a giant brown trout intent on grabbing the whitefish. The big brown grabbed the whitefish for an instant before it pulled free. He made another swipe at it before he spooked from the boat and swam slowly away. We couldn't believe it. That whitefish was at least 14 inches long and the brown could have swallowed it whole.

There have been some monster browns landed, but the biggest ones are usually caught on bait or large deep-running lures. That doesn't mean you can't get big ones on your fly rod, however. You've just got to figure out how to cast a fly that looks and acts like a 14-inch whitefish.

When the Salmon Fly hatch comes off, the larger browns and rainbows move into the banks to pick off the migrating nymphs. There are lots of deep undercut banks and rock ledges which offer great cover. The larger fish like to hold as tight in as possible, so you can't be afraid to lose a fly or two from casting too close to the bank. Often an inch or two will make the difference.

WARM RIVER TO ASHTON

Warm River is a major tributary to the Henry's Fork, and, along with nearby Robinson Creek, it is a fun stream to fish in its own right. One of the things that I like most about fishing these two streams is that you have a chance to get a "grand slam" with four species of trout—rainbow, brown, cutthroat, and brook.

Warm River is important to the Henry's Fork for a number of reasons. First, it is a clean, spring-fed stream. Because it's a spring creek, it has a more constant water temperature regime that is important for fry survival and provides clean gravel ideal for spawning success. The rainbows move up in February and March, and the browns spawn in October and November. Warm River opens for fishing with the general season on Memorial Day weekend and closes September 30 to protect the fall spawners.

This constant water temperature also has an effect on the Henry's Fork below the confluence. Early in the season, when the Salmon Flies come off, the water entering the Henry's Fork is considerably warmer than the main river. This causes the big stoneflies to emerge a little earlier than on the rest of the river.

The section from Warm River down to the Ashton Reservoir can be an angling circus on Memorial Day weekend. This is also opening day weekend and the Salmon Fly hatch is usually well under way. The Henry's Fork is often the only show in town, because most other regional rivers are high and muddy with snow runoff. One way to avoid the crowds on this section is to try to fish it during the week.

One way to gauge the Salmon Fly hatch in this part of the river, is to check the chokecherry blossoms. Along Ashton Hill, there are scads of chokecherry trees. Over the years I've noticed that the chokecherry trees are always in blossom at the same time the Salmon Fly hatch is occurring. If there are lots of blossoms, you will probably have good dry-fly fishing. If the blossoms aren't in full bloom, nymphs will likely be your best bet.

The section from Warm River to Ashton provides some of the most consistent fishing on a year-round basis. The Golden Stones and smaller Yellow Sally stoneflies provide excellent dry-fly opportunities throughout the month of June. There are some very heavy caddis hatches as well.

Because it gets a good mix of both aquatic insects and ter-restrials, attractor patterns are productive throughout the sea-son. I like downwing patterns such as Trudes and Stimulators, as well as the modern foam-bodied hoppers and ants. One of my favorite tactics is to fish a trailing nymph below a dropper pattern. I like to tie on a beadhead Prince Nymph or Pheasant Tail about three feet below the top fly. This is effective for working the undercut banks, the riffles, and the pocket water. In the deeper runs you can use the same kind of deep nymph tactics described for the Box Canyon.

While most of the trout are small—in the 10- to 14-inch range—you have a great shot at getting a big fish at any time of the year. One day Kim Martin was guiding an older fellow who had a serious heart condition. His two middle-aged sons were with another guide in a second boat. While Kim was rowing across to change banks, a big brown came out and slammed the dry fly. It was a tremendous battle as they chased the big trout down the river in the boat. By the time they finally got it to the net the old fellow was as exhausted as the trout. It was a good seven pounds. When they got back up to the shop we knew we had serious trouble. His heart was really acting up, so we called the paramedics. Eventually he was air lifted to the hospital in Rexburg.

I called the hospital to see how he was doing the next morning. I talked to one of his sons and he told me his father was doing fine. All he could talk about was his big brown. In fact he wanted the boys to go back up and fish with us a couple more days until he was released from the hospital. He said he'd enjoy his recuperation a lot more knowing they were fishing. He knew his heart would eventually get him, he said, and if he could choose two ways to go, that big brown was one of them.

ASHTON RESERVOIR

Ashton Reservoir is an enticing piece of water. Drive across the Wendall Bridge, look downstream, and see its nice, slow backwater, and you can envision dry-fly angling to fish that are gulping on the surface of the lake. But it's not worth wasting your time on this reservoir. It's not a very productive fishery.

IDFG stocks the reservoir very heavily with hatchery catchables. Local farm workers fish from the rock bluffs just where the river backs up above the reservoir. They make good use of a beer can. After they drink the contents, they wrap about 50 yards of mono line around it and tie a hook on and bait it with a fat worm. They swing the worm around their head and sling it. It is amazing how far they can cast and they really nail those hatchery rainbows.

There is good wading water above the highway bridge where you can find plenty of action. The hatchery trout move up into this stretch and you can usually catch them hand over fist. It is a good place to go if you want to give some young fly fishers or novices a chance to catch fish. You'll have the best luck swinging a wet fly down and across. I like a Renegade or soft hackle wet fly for this. Now and again you'll hook a nice wild brown or rainbow in the process.

Ashton Reservoir to St. Anthony

Ashton Reservoir itself may not have much value as a fishery, but below Ashton Dam, you have the classic tail-water, with lots of riffles, flats, runs, and islands. While hatches aren't as important here as on the Railroad Ranch, they are still excellent. Like most tailwaters, the dam provides a more constant water temperature and the reservoir enriches the water. The Henry's Fork below Ashton Dam is as productive as Box Canyon and Railroad Ranch.

There are some huge trout in this section. The river is on the general season schedule from Ashton Reservoir down to Vernon Bridge, about 2½ miles. From the bridge down to St. Anthony it is open year-round. The stretch below the Ashton Dam is closed part of the year to allow trout to spawn unmolested in this reach.

The Chester Backwater is a great place to fish the Gray Drake hatch that usually starts about the third week of June. (Photo by Mike Lawson)

The year-round fishing provides those of us who endure the long Idaho winters with some great fishing opportunities. The midges start to produce great dry-fly fishing in October and continue right through the teeth of the winter. When I was young, I went fishing every Saturday, no matter what the weather. I always caught fish, but as I got older I got tired of breaking ice out of my guides.

Good hatches of Blue-Winged Olive mayflies and Grannom caddisflies start in the spring. By then the fishing pressure starts to get heavy, especially on weekends, but it doesn't seem to affect the fishery. In fact, there are more trout per mile from Ashton Dam to St. Anthony than in any other stretch of the Henry's Fork. There is a good number of fish in the 14- to 18-inch range, and they are really hot, well-conditioned fish.

This section also has some exceptional mayfly hatches. There is an extraordinary Gray Drake spinner fall in June, but there are no Brown Drakes. There are good hatches of Green

Drakes, Pale Morning Duns, Flavs, and Mahogany Duns, but there aren't many Tricos or *Callibaetis*. There are also some of the heaviest caddisfly hatches I've ever witnessed on any trout water, with blanket flights of Spotted Sedge and Little Sister Sedge on summer evenings. It's hard to find rivers that have the kind of habitat that will support a heavy Salmon Fly hatch, heavy caddisfly activity, *and* heavy mayfly activity. But this part of the river has it all and offers good dry-fly fishing almost all year long.

The Gray Drake hatch occurs in virtually the entire stretch of river from Ashton Dam down to well below the town of St. Anthony. My favorite place to fish the Gray Drake hatch is downstream in a little irrigation reservoir called the Chester Backwater. There is a little diversion dam that backs the river up for about a mile. This is all really flat, slow moving, deep water and the spinners really come into this area. Sometimes you need a boat, but you can fish this effectively from shore as well. They typically start coming about two o'clock in the afternoon and really peak around 8:00 p.m. The Gray Drake hatch shows up around the third week of June and the egg-laying lasts into early July. The average size of the Gray Drake spinner is between size 10 and size 12. They carpet the water so heavily that the fish school up to feed on them.

When the Gray Drake hatch is at its height, the fish cruise and sip spinners off the surface. And the fish usually aren't very selective. My favorite fly is a size-10 Parachute Adams. It sits low on the surface film yet it is easy to see, especially later in the evening. You can even use a much larger fly because the spinners tend to clump together, falling on the water during the mating process. Sometimes the trout actually seem to key on these clumps of huge mayflies.

The Henry's Fork flows right through downtown St. Anthony—if a town that has only one stoplight has a "downtown." The Gray Drakes drive all non-anglers nuts for a week or so. The flies congregate all over town. Sometimes the hatch is so thick that merchants in St. Anthony have to sweep the flies off the sidewalk.

One of my friends lives just down the street on the river. A few years ago, when his daughter got married, they decided to have a backyard reception in late June. When he told me about it I told him it was going to be a big mistake. He couldn't understand why. By the time we got to the reception everything had been moved indoors. I've never heard such a beautiful mayfly called so many terrible names. Large mayflies covered the salads, hors d'oeuvres, and punch. They were in everyone's hair. The decorations were covered with bugs. The bride's gown looked like it was made from white flypaper. The Gray Drakes literally destroyed the reception.

ST. ANTHONY TO THE SNAKE RIVER

The Henry's Fork below St. Anthony is different than the water above St. Anthony. I find the section below town some of the most interesting trout water of the entire river system. There are numerous channels which braid through great cottonwood bottoms. Pools, riffles, runs, and flats offer a wide variety of fishing opportunities.

Access is difficult because private land surrounds much of the river, but the river bottom itself is owned mostly by the Bureau of Land Management. Two good points to get on include the old railroad bridge just below St. Anthony and the bridge at the Parker Highway. The Parker Highway bridge is of historical interest because it is near where Andrew Henry, who first explored the river that now bears his name, built a fur trading fort. He spent the winter of 1810–1811 here and narrowly avoided starvation before spring finally arrived. There is a marker just south of the bridge. The actual location of the old encampment is about 400 yards upriver.

Below St. Anthony the Henry's Fork flows into channels that braid through cottonwood bottoms, offering a variety of fishing opportunities in pools, riffles, runs, and flats. (Photo by Mike Lawson)

It is possible to float several sections of this stretch but you really need to know the water. The access points are very tricky and the river changes from year to year. The best channel one year may have a large cottonwood tree blocking navigation the following year.

The first mile or so below St. Anthony is good wading. Early in the season, however, during the Gray Drake hatch, it can be downright treacherous. After the spring runoff ends, the water drops to a more comfortable level. As summer progresses, a lot of water gets diverted for irrigation. During drought the river can slow to a trickle, seriously affecting the trout population.

This isn't match-the-hatch water. You can usually get plenty of trout using an attractor pattern, such as a Royal Wulff, Humpy, Double Wing, or Trude along with a bead-head dropper. Large rubber-leg nymphs like Girdle Bugs and Yuk Bugs can also produce some nice trout. Bob Lamm, a well-known Henry's Fork guide, landed a rainbow which measured 30 inches in length and 18 inches in girth on a Girdle Bug twitched off the bank in a small side channel. Streamers are effective on larger fish, especially late in the season (October–November) when the browns get more aggressive. During late summer hoppers fished along the undercut banks might draw some monster trout.

When I was growing up near St. Anthony, before I was old enough to drive, I frequently rode my bike to this part of the river. Almost all of the trout were native cutthroats and some of them got quite large. Now brown trout make up more than 50 percent of the population. There are still some fine cutthroats down near the confluence of the Teton River above Rexburg. The Teton still gets a good cutthroat spawning run.

MAJOR TRIBUTARIES

There are several important Henry's Fork tributaries. Fall River and Teton River are two of the most important. Both of these streams are blue-ribbon trout streams in their own right and would probably be better known if they didn't flow in the shadow of the Henry's Fork.

BUFFALO RIVER

The Buffalo is one of the best family fishing areas around. The wading is easy, the access is good, and there are plenty of small eager trout. The Buffalo River joins the Henry's Fork just below the Island Park Dam and its greatest contribution to the fishing in the region undoubtedly has been to save the Box Canyon from total extinction. After the dam was built in the early 1930s the stream flow was totally cut off, sometimes for the entire winter. During those times the river was sustained by the flow of the Buffalo River.

There was also a small hydro dam on the Buffalo which prevented migration from the Box Canyon into its rich

Warm River is a spring creek that offers brook trout fishing tailor made for introducing kids to fly fishing. (Photo by Mike Lawson)

spawning waters. When this project came up for relicensing under the FERC requirements, a fish ladder was installed which allows trout to once again move into the fertile spawning grounds of the Buffalo River.

While the Buffalo River has outstanding spawning and overwintering trout habitat, it is not productive enough to produce large resident trout. It is a fairly short, high-volume spring creek only a few miles in length. Buffalo Campground near Pond's Lodge on Highway 20 provides good access. This part of the river is heavily stocked with hatchery catchables, but you can walk upstream a mile or so and get into some great fishing for small brook trout.

WARM RIVER

Like the Buffalo River, Warm River is a spring creek which offers great fishing opportunities for smaller trout, but it's greatest contribution is the spawning and overwintering habitat for the trout of the Henry's Fork.

The upper Warm River has lots of beaver ponds and pools full of wild brook trout. These are all small fish—a large one won't top 8 inches—but they are tailor-made for granddad and a bunch of grandchildren. It doesn't matter what fly you throw out. There will usually be a brookie on it soon after it hits the water. I remember the days I spent fishing with my grandpa on this quiet little stream and not much has changed in three generations.

The canyon stretch of Warm River parallels the Henry's Fork near Mesa Falls. It also requires a steep climb down to the river. The old railroad track bed follows Warm River from its source to the confluence with the Henry's Fork. This makes an ideal trail for hiking or riding a mountain bike to get to some remote water.

There is a small Forest Service campground just above the confluence on the Mesa Falls Scenic Highway. It's a great family spot and is popular with the locals. The fish and game department stocks the campground area with hatchery rainbows, but hike up the trail a few hundred yards and you get into wild browns, rainbows, and brookies.

FALL RIVER

Fall River starts in the southwestern corner of Yellowstone National Park and flows west until it joins the Henry's Fork, a distance of almost fifty miles. The headwaters, including the Bechler River and Boundary Creek, offer an exceptional backcountry experience for quality trout. You need to pick up a fishing permit at the Bechler Ranger Station to fish this water.

Fall River cascades its way out of Yellowstone, offering one of the most picturesque settings in the area at Cave Falls. There is great fishing for small rainbows in this stretch but you'll be lucky to catch one over 12 inches. The remoteness of the upper Fall River offers an opportunity to explore, get away from the crowds, and find quality fishing in the stretch from the Yellowstone Park boundary through national forest land.

Below the forest boundary, Fall River flows through private land so you'll need permission unless you enter the river at one of many access points. The Fall River, unlike any other river in the area, is closed to commercial boating. Guides cannot legally float fish clients on the river.

Lower Fall River has an excellent population of wild rainbows. Because it is a freestone stream, the growing season is much shorter than the Henry's Fork . Fall River carries heavy snow runoff in the spring and gets cold and icy in the winter. There are some big trout, however, and it is not uncommon to hook a fat rainbow that will run well over 20 inches.

TETON RIVER

The Teton River is a spring-fed stream which starts near Victor, Idaho, just over the mountain from Jackson Hole, Wyoming. The upper stretch is classic spring creek water in every sense of the word. Most of the land surrounding the river is private, so you need to ask permission unless you park at one of the public access points. In Idaho it is legal to walk up or down the stream as long as you stay within the high water mark.

The upper Teton gets many of the same hatches you find on the Railroad Ranch of the Henry's Fork. Probably the best is the Pale Morning Dun, which emerges from late June until mid-August. There are plenty of Blue-Winged Olives, Tricos, and other mayflies to keep the dry-fly fishing good throughout the season.

The Teton also has a deep canyon section. The access is limited. This is where the ill-fated Teton Dam was constructed. The dam failed in June 1976, the first year it was in operation. It totally flooded the small town of Sugar City, where I grew up, as well as the surrounding communities.

Of course, the flood also totally changed the structure of the canyon, but there are still some very good fishing spots. The Teton River is special because it still supports a decent population of cutthroat trout, once native to all of the Henry's Fork drainage.

The Teton River is unique in another respect. Its forks diverge instead of converging. The north fork flows to the Henry's Fork near the town of Sugar City, while the south fork flows through a good golf course at Rexburg before it joins the Henry's Fork. Both of these forks offer marginal fishing opportunity because they get dewatered in the summer during the irrigation season.

WHITEFISH
CAUGHT AND CUSSED, BUT MISUNDERSTOOD

The Rocky Mountain Whitefish is a game fish, native to the Henry's Fork and other rivers in the Rocky Mountain region. They take flies readily, put up a respectable battle, and reach decent size. In fact, the average whitefish will fight much better than the popular cutthroat trout. In spite of that, this native game fish often gets a bad rap from visiting fly fishers.

Fishermen will come up from the river with a glazed look in their eyes, and they'll say, "The Henry's Fork is the worse whitefish river I have ever seen." The whitefish really get into the hatches. When the mayflies come off, you'll see big schools of whitefish rising, and it can really be a real headache for an angler who doesn't want to catch them. You can learn how to avoid whitefish by learning how to catch them. Even though their feeding habits are similar to trout and they eat many of the same types of food, there are some distinct differences.

Whitefish are a schooling fish. Even the big ones like to hang together. Large trout, on the other hand, like to pick

out holding areas where they can find solitude, often running all competitors away. Whitefish tend to hold in different
parts of the river than trout, and when they feed they rise a
little differently than a trout does. You will find whitefish
either in the riffle areas or out in the deeper water of
Harriman State Park.

Watch the rise forms. Each time a whitefish rises, it
comes all the way to the surface to take a fly and goes back
down. As a result, whitefish have kind of a porpoise rise;
they come up and roll right over and back down they go.
When trout are up and feeding, they'll hold just under the
surface and just poke their noses out. The differences in the
rise forms are distinctive. Also, when I see a lot of fish rising
in the same area in an erratic sequence, I usually assume they
are whitefish. Trout like to get into a more regular rhythm.

But don't sell the whitefish short. They are excellent quarry
for novice fly fishermen. I took my son, Shaun, when he first
started fly fishing, to areas where lots of whitefish were feeding
on Brown Drakes. Whitefish, because they are such frequent
risers, offer the angler excellent dry-fly opportunities.

But if you really want to avoid whitefish, learn to identify
the big trout rises and concentrate your efforts on fishing
where the larger trout are, and you'll pretty much avoid the
whitefish. Big trout usually won't feed right in the middle of
a school of surface-feeding whitefish.

Another way to avoid catching whitefish is to fish tight
to structure, like the banks, trees, or rocks. Whitefish tend to
stay closer to the middle. If you stalk bank sippers and fish
close to shore, you're going to avoid most of the whitefish.

One other way to avoid whitefish is to avoid mayfly
hatches. Fish the caddis hatches because whitefish normally
do not key on caddisflies on the surface. The caddis move a
bit too quickly to be readily caught in the small, underslung
mouth of the whitefish. Of course, by choosing this tactic,

you stand the chance of missing some really good trout feeding on mayfly hatches.

If you are blind fishing with nymphs, it is almost impossible to avoid catching whitefish. They feed heavily on immature aquatic insects. There is actually a special whitefish season on some streams. They are excellent eating and you don't need to feel guilty about keeping a few. They are so prolific that their healthy population won't be easily harmed by throwing a couple in the frying pan. They also are delicious smoked—much better than trout.

Many anglers don't realize what a blessing it is to catch a few whitefish occasionally. They require the cleanest, purest water. When the water quality is degraded, whitefish are one of the first species to disappear. The Henry's Fork fishery declined in the late eighties and early nineties. Henry's Fork regulars first noticed a decline in the trout population. This was later confirmed by the Idaho Fish and Game Department. When I look back, had I been more on the ball I would have known much sooner, because we weren't catching as many whitefish. At the time, we thought it was great. Since then I've gained a greater appreciation for this most special game fish of the Rocky Mountains.

CHAPTER 2

Seasons of the River

INTER

I wouldn't make a special trip to fish the Henry's Fork in December, January, or February. The weather in southeastern Idaho can be down right awful. Below zero temperatures are common in and around St. Anthony and Ashton. Another problem is that there isn't much water legally open for fishing. Idaho is not as progressive as its neighbors, and doesn't offer many year-round fishing opportunities. The general season opens on Memorial Day weekend and closes the end of November.

There is a stretch of river below Ashton that is open all year and it can provide some exceptional fishing if the weather is right. Not only is the Henry's Fork a large spring creek, but there is a tailwater below the dam at Ashton that doesn't freeze, no matter how cold the air temperature is.

I remember one day in early January freezing my butt off with my brother Rick. We were sitting off the point of an island just below the Ashton Dam, hoping to bag a few late-season mallards which were concentrating on the river because everything else was frozen solid. The air temperature wasn't much above zero. There weren't many ducks flying and, to make matters worse, there were dozens of trout rising among our ice-laden decoys. It was quite a sight. The trout were feeding on midges which seem to emerge from mid-October until late April, regardless of what the air temperature is. It seems the colder it gets, the more the midges like it.

You're nuts if you plan to make a special trip to the Henry's Fork just to fish, but if you like to ski, don't forget your fly rod. The Henry's Fork isn't that far from some darned good skiing. Grand Targhee offers some of the best around and it is only forty-five minutes away. Jackson Hole is two hours, Sun Valley three and a half hours, and Big Sky, Montana, is about a two and a half hour drive from St. Anthony.

If the weather isn't too miserable you can have some great dry-fly fishing during the winter months. You might have to break the ice out of your guides, but if you can stand it, the trout will usually be rising. The dry-fly fishing is best when the sky is overcast. The midges really seem to come out when the weather is cloudy. The bigger trout don't rise as freely to midges. Most of the fish will be 10 to 14 inches, but it can be a lot of fun with a light action rod.

Bigger trout can be taken throughout the winter on nymphs and streamers. There are some really nice browns throughout the section below Ashton. The percentage of browns increases the further you get below St. Anthony. Spawning season also increases your odds of getting a real big fish. The browns spawn in November and early December; the rainbows spawn in February and March. The best tactic is to make them mad. Big brightly colored Zonkers, Clousers, and other bright streamers will often

Odds of catching a big fish when winter fishing near St. Anthony are increased during brown trout spawning season in November and early December and rainbow spawning in February and March. (Photo by Mike Lawson)

entice them to attack. Sometimes an egg pattern will also produce good fish.

My favorite nymph for winter season angling is a Prince Nymph. I have one fly box completely filled with Prince Nymphs from size 8 through 16. I tie plenty of them with beadheads, using tungsten beads to get them to sink quicker. In addition I tie a few with rubber legs and others with red wire twisted through the peacock herl. When you add them up, there isn't room for anything but Prince Nymphs. Sometimes I use Pheasant Tail and Hare's Ear nymphs.

I don't like to kill fish to eat, but I must confess, its hard to beat a pan-sized trout caught from the cold waters of winter. I slip down behind my house in St. Anthony about once a year, usually in February, with the specific purpose of bringing home a couple of keepers. The fish are usually still wiggling when they hit the hot skillet. Some of the local people occasionally label us as elitist fly-fishing purists. The taste of a firm trout fillet cooked fresh in the dead of winter is my way of proving them wrong.

 **PRING**

Pre-runoff, from early spring until mid-May is one of the best times to fish any western trout stream, including the Henry's Fork. Even though the Henry's Fork is mainly a spring-fed river, there are tributary streams which carry enough snowmelt to muddy the stretch of the river that is open year-round. I don't recommend that you plan on fishing the river from early May until the general fishing season opens on Memorial Day weekend. There is usually a two- or three-week period after runoff starts and before the Salmon Flies start to emerge, that the fishing is blown out because of spring runoff. But late winter and early spring can produce some of the best fishing of the year.

In March we start getting really good hatches of *Baetis* mayflies, commonly known as Blue-Winged Olives. By the time the *Baetis* show up, the trout are already accustomed to feeding on midges on the surface, so it's an easy transition to the larger (size-18) *Baetis*. The larger trout begin to show more interest in surface feeding as the water temperatures rise and the mayflies start to emerge.

After the *Baetis*, there is a good hatch of Western March Browns (*Rithrogena morrisoni*). These big (size-12) mayflies can produce some exciting dry-fly angling. The fish are already tuned into the smaller Blue-Winged Olives so it doesn't take many of the bigger *Rithrogena* mayflies to really get some big trout up to the surface.

Good caddis hatches start in April and continue right into summer. The best is the Grannom (*Brachycentrus americanus* and *B. occidentalis*). The spring caddis hatches can be intense, with trout rising all over the river. Ironically, the Montana rivers seem to get more attention when it comes to early season caddis fishing. The Mother's Day Caddis hatch on the Yellowstone is legendary. Unfortunately, the Yellowstone River, like many other western trout rivers in April and May is often high, dirty, and out of sorts. The Henry's Fork, in contrast, is clear and fishable for the Grannom, at least until early May.

In the early spring, the water is still fairly cold; during the morning hours, you don't get the hatches. If you arrive at the stream in the morning and there is no surface activity, usually you can catch some nice fish on streamers or nymphs. I prefer streamers myself. I like to fish with a two fly rig, with a streamer as the top fly and a large wet fly tied in about 18 inches below the streamer.

A good combination would be a silver or gold Zonker for the top fly with a Woolly Bugger below it using a sink-tip line. I like to use a size-4 Zonker and a smaller Woolly Bugger, size 8 or 10. I cast straight across and mend the line a little bit and then just let the current swing the flies downstream. I don't strip them at all until the flies are well below me, and then I just strip it back a short distance to start the cast again. The trout will usually hit just before or at the end of the swing.

If you fish nymphs this time of year, add plenty of weight and just feel the fly bouncing on the bottom. When the trout pick it up, it will just stop. You won't feel a solid strike. For most people, an indicator can be a great help. Make sure to place the indicator far enough up the leader to compensate for the depth and velocity of the water. One and one half times the depth of the water is a good place to start. I personally like buoyant yarn as opposed to hard foam indicators but it's a matter of personal preference. As to fly selection, the best choices this time of year are stonefly nymphs or bead-head nymphs. Again, it's hard to beat a Prince Nymph.

Another tactic to consider when trout are feeding during the emergence of a mayfly or caddis hatch is to use a nymph or pupa dropper just under the dry fly. For mayflies, use a Pheasant Tail of appropriate size tied about a foot below the dry fly. For caddisflies, use the same tactic with a Deep Sparkle Pupa. You'll usually catch more fish on the dropper, especially if you're fishing during a caddis hatch. Be sure to keep the dropper fairly close to the dry fly. Sometimes it even helps to grease up the dropper so it fishes flush in the surface film.

 **UMMER**

Even though the first day of summer isn't until June 21, the Salmon Fly hatch really marks the start of the summer season on the Henry's Fork. It is always in full swing somewhere on the river as it moves up the river a few miles a day. The lower river is usually high and a bit off-color, providing a perfect opportunity to catch trout feeding on the emerging stonefly nymphs just off the bank.

While many visiting anglers chase the Salmon Fly hatch up the river, there are good hatches of mayflies and caddisflies in the river above and just below the Island Park Reservoir at Last Chance. No matter how heavy the spring runoff, this stretch is a near-perfect spring creek and runs clear and clean year-round. The angling pressure on these sections of the river is usually light, especially during the middle of the week. Most visiting anglers either plan their trip around the Salmon Fly hatch or wait until after June 15 when the Harriman State Park section of the river is open for fishing.

The Henry's Fork has one of the earliest Salmon Fly hatches in the Rocky Mountain region beginning late May to early June. (Photo by Glenda Bradshaw)

Things really start to heat up around Last Chance by June 15. The crowds pour in because that's when the seven-mile section within the Harriman State Park is open to fishing. The first day these notoriously selective trout are relatively stupid, because they haven't been fished for more than seven months. They usually wise up by the second day. Another reason crowds pour into Harriman is that they hope to catch the famous Green Drake (*Ephemerella grandis*) hatch.

One problem with the Green Drake hatch is that it is really inconsistent. It's a great hatch when it's good, but it's really hard to hit it just right. And when it's not just right, it can be really tough to fish. In fact, during the same period as the Green Drake hatch, there are more species of insects hatching on the river than at any other time of the entire year. On a typical day at Green Drake time, you'll see Pale Morning Dun (*Ephemerella inermis*) spinners and some Green Drake spinners first thing in the morning. Later the

Pale Morning Duns will start coming off. If you're lucky the Green Drakes will hatch from about eleven o'clock to one o'clock. By midafternoon, there should be some little Blue-Winged Olive (*Baetis*) mayflies starting to come off. In the late afternoon and evening, you can have Spotted Sedge and Long-Horn Sedge caddisflies, several species of mayfly spinners, and a few big Brown Drakes. There is plenty to keep you busy even if you don't even see a Green Drake.

A few years ago I was fishing down in the Ranch with my friend, René Harrop, hoping to find a good Green Drake hatch. I was fishing a special Green Drake Nymph of my own creation in anticipation of the hatch. René was casting dries to some big rising trout that were feeding on small mayflies. It wasn't long before I connected with a big rainbow which immediately went crashing upstream through the weeds and broke off.

An hour later René yelled for me to come up and look at a nice trout he had just landed. It was a big fish but not exceptional enough to warrant a one-hundred-yard trip upstream, but I reeled in and waded upstream anyway. René wouldn't have disturbed my fishing unless it was something very important. When I got up to him he had a fine rainbow of 20 inches cradled in his net with a tiny No-Hackle hooked through the eye of a nymph which was broken off in the trout's upper jaw. René couldn't believe it. He had landed the trout by hooking the eye of a fly that another angler had lost to this great fish. Even more astonishing was that the nymph was my own which had been broken off only an hour earlier. Honest. I even have René as a witness.

Crowds have been an issue on the Henry's Fork since the early seventies. Back then you couldn't pick up a national sporting magazine without reading about the river. It was also a time when fly fishing was becoming more fashionable.

The tremendously high quality of the fishing also pulled crowds onto the river. There were more big trout in the Ranch than at any other time in my memory. Why it didn't seem to bother so many anglers to fish so close together was difficult for me to understand. Fortunately, there has never been a time when the river was so crowded that you couldn't walk a mile or so and get some good water to yourself.

I deal with the crowds on the Ranch by not fishing there during the crowded time. You usually won't see me out there in late June. The Henry's Fork is almost one hundred miles long, not including its four major tributaries. There is plenty of good access all the way down to the confluence near Rexburg and the fishing is good on the entire river. I love the Green Drake hatch but not enough to share it with one hundred other anglers. I'll head for the lower river between Ashton and St. Anthony. There is good Green Drake water there, and I can always find a reasonable amount of solitude.

My favorite summer period on the river is from late July through early August, because the river isn't crowded and there are still some pretty good mayfly and caddisfly hatches. And, maybe even more importantly, the terrestrials really start to play a big role. When most anglers talk terrestrials, they think of big hoppers and explosive rises. You can get that on the Henry's Fork but ants, beetles, and small crickets are frequently more important.

Another midsummer bonus is that the lakes fish the best during the months of July and August, especially if you want to try to get some dry-fly fishing on Island Park Reservoir. The lake was formed in the 1930s when Island Park Dam was constructed. It is a shallow lake with miles of shallow flats with thick weed beds. There is great access from the west side of the lake. The trout grow fat and sassy with plenty of leeches, nymphs, and bait fish to feed on.

Dry-fly fishing is best on Island Park Reservoir in July and August, beginning with damselflies and intensifying with the Callibaetis *hatch. (Photo by Mike Lawson)*

The best dry-fly fishing occurs when the damselflies start to emerge in July, and intensifies with the *Callibaetis* hatch. The dry-fly fishing may be a little more predictable further north on Hebgen Lake, but in Island Park you always have the chance to hook a double-digit rainbow on a dry fly.

 UTUMN

If there was any one season of the year that I would pick as my personal favorite to fish the Henry's Fork it would be the fall. The fishing is good, probably better than any other time of the year, and it isn't as crowded (although we see more people on the river in the fall than we used to). There are some excellent mayfly hatches that go right into the first part of November—two types of Blue-Winged Olives, Mahogany Duns, *Callibaetis*, and even a good Trico hatch.

There are also some great late season caddisfly hatches, and a fair number of terrestrials.

The dry-fly fishing is good not only in the Harriman Park. It is also exceptional on the long flats of the lower river where large rainbows and browns settle in the slots between the weed beds to feed on the huge mayfly hatches.

On the lower river, the brown trout become much more aggressive in the autumn months in preparation for spawning. They load up on food before the rigorous spawning season begins. The rainbows also feed more intensely with the approach of the winter season.

Streamer tactics are the most popular for the brown trout. Early morning and late evening hours are often the best times to entice a big brown. They also seem to be much more active on cool, cloudy days. On warm Indian Summer days you can sometimes get the browns to smash a large attractor dry fly skated across the surface. I like the foam-bodied, Chernobyl Ant–style patterns, with long rubber legs. You can also use a two-fly rig, an attractor dry fly with a nymph dropper, for plenty of hot action.

October is the best month to catch the most and largest trout in Henry's Lake. The brook trout start to concentrate near the mouths of the spawning creeks in mid-September. By October they are usually packed into these areas along with cutthroat and hybrid trout. You need to use a sinking-line technique to fish Henry's Lake. The average depth of the lake is about 12 feet, so a type 2 or type 3 full sinking line is needed to get the fly to the proper depth. If you're really after a trophy-sized brookie, in the four- to five-pound class, get up early in the morning. That first hour before the sun breaks above the horizon is the magic time, even if you have to break some ice out of your guides.

CHAPTER 3

Salmon Flies

*T*he secret is out on the Salmon Fly hatch. For many years, there weren't a lot of people who traveled to fish this hatch on the Henry's Fork. Has that ever changed. Now you see boat trailers in every parking lot with license plates from Idaho, Utah, Wyoming, Montana, Colorado, and more. Not too long ago the locals had the river pretty much to themselves until the Railroad Ranch opened in mid-June.

It is easy to see why things changed. The Henry's Fork is the only show in town in late May and early June. Most of the other rivers in the Rocky Mountain region are flushed with snowmelt, high and dirty, and unfishable for the most part. The Henry's Fork also runs high but stays clear, offering perfect conditions to fish the Salmon Flies. Another factor is the substantial increase in the number of people who own drift boats or pontoon boats. A few years ago most drift boats were owned by fishing guides.

Salmon Flies are large members of the stonefly family, with adults sometimes reaching two inches in length. The robust dark nymphs live for up to four years before they emerge. Prior to emergence they concentrate at the stream bank where they crawl out to emerge. The nymphs attach to rocks, branches, and other objects where the transformation from nymph to adult takes place. Then they mate and swarm over the river to lay their eggs. It is a spectacle to see these giant aquatic insects buzzing over the water like miniature B-17s.

The nymphs are what the trout are most interested in. You usually won't be able to get the fish to consistently take the adults on the surface until the nymphs have stopped migrating. I've checked stomach contents and the fish are usually packed full of nymphs before they start looking for the adults. They can quickly fill up on these giant insects. For that reason it is often better to fish with nymphs up river ahead of the hatch or behind it. You can get some good fishing right in the middle of the hatch, but it's a lot more difficult to find where these fish are really working the adults. They might be tearing the water up at 10:00 a.m., but by noon they act like a bunch of couch potatoes who just finished watching the Super Bowl, slouching back with an empty bag of chips and a case of empty beer cans.

The Salmon Fly hatch is important up and down the river, from where Fall River comes in, all the way up to Coffee Pot Rapids. Generally, May 25 is the time that you can usually plan on seeing some. The first Salmon Flies usually start to come out about May 25.

The Salmon Fly hatch on the Henry's Fork is unlike any that I have seen on other rivers. On most rivers, once the hatch starts, there is a steady, more or less predictable, upstream migration. The Henry's Fork has so many temperature variations throughout its length that you get Salmon Flies in different parts of the river at the same time. For example, the Buffalo River, a spring creek, feeds the river at the top of the Box Canyon. We always get crazed anglers coming to our shop shouting, "The Salmon Flies are out! The Salmon Flies are out!" Before everyone dives for their cars, we tell them to hold on. The big flies emerge just below the Buffalo a week to ten days before they come off in the rest of the Box Canyon because the temperature is slightly warmer at the confluence of the Buffalo River.

An important key to success in fishing Salmon Fly imitations is knowing when to fish dry flies and when to fish nymphs. I like to start by looking at the willows and rocks on the stream bank. If I see a lot of nymphal shucks and no adult flies, then I know I probably missed the hatch. That doesn't mean I'll leave and look further upstream. In fact that could mean that the trout are finally hungry again with those big, fat, tasty flies still on their minds. I will cover all of the likely looking holding water with a large dry Salmon Fly pattern. You don't need to just fish along the banks. In fact, I've caught more big trout out in the middle of the runs, especially at the end of the hatch.

If you see nymphs that are still emerging, maybe just a few adult flies (in the evenings, you will actually see nymphs hatching into adults), it's a good place to fish the nymphs. Don't be afraid to fish the nymphs in shallow water, right on the bank. A common misconception is that you need to use large nymphs that resemble spark plugs both in weight and size. While I carry some heavily weighted nymphs, I also carry some lightweights that I can fish in shallow water without dredging out half of the rocks in the river. If the trout are really keyed into the migrating nymphs, you're going to find the fastest action of the Salmon Fly hatch.

I would rather catch one big trout on a dry Salmon Fly pattern than a dozen on a weighted nymph. You can keep your eye on the water and occasionally see a trout bust one of the adults, but for the most part, you won't be fishing to rising fish. You just have to cover all of the good holding water. That's the fun of it. It's like the trout have their eye on you and as soon as you lose concentration, they're on your fly. It can make you jump right out of your wading shoes.

FISHING NYMPHS

You don't need to fish fancy nymphs. When I worked as a fishing guide in West Yellowstone in the early seventies our two best nymphs were a dark Brooks Stone and a Black Rubber Legs in size 4 or 6. That hasn't changed in over twenty years. The advantage is that they are easy and quick to tie, and less expensive to buy than those fancy patterns that look like they're going to crawl out of your fly box. Plan to lose a lot of them, especially if you are fishing out of a boat. If you aren't losing them, you probably aren't fishing them right.

Early in the season fish heavily weighted nymphs deep in the runs. The Salmon Fly nymphs start to get active on the lower Henry's Fork in early May. Over the next few weeks they migrate towards the bank. If I feel I'm a week ahead of the emergence I like to fish the deep fast water.

Sometimes, if you use something that is a little different color you can move fish. Stonefly nymphs in both green and olive have proven to be effective during the Salmon Fly hatch. One good pattern is a Rubber Legs with a tan and gold variegated body with brown rubber legs.

I have had some good days fishing a pale-colored nymph, even a cream, during the Salmon Fly hatch. The only reason I tried that is some of the biologists who have done studies on the river told me that when they're diving, the nymphs appeared to be cream colored. Their gills are cream and they really stand out. I don't use a cream colored nymph very often, but there are times when it can really work. I'll often use it as a dropper fly, fishing two nymphs at one time.

A two-nymph rig can be productive above Ashton during the Salmon Fly hatch. (Photo by Mike Lawson)

This is a good tactic if you're just not doing well with the traditional stonefly nymphs. In fact, when I'm fishing the Salmon Fly hatch, I usually fish a two-fly system, both with nymphs and dries. When it comes to multi-fly systems, though, I'm a piker compared to Jack Dennis. I once fished the hatch with him above Ashton and he had a string of flies that stretched from the boat to the bank, covering all of the water in between. The rig included several dry flies and nymphs. Amazingly, he could control all of those flies, both in the air and in the water. Don't try that at home.

Day in and day out, all season long, Salmon Fly nymphs will catch fish. Remember, the nymphs live for up to four years. That means they are always in the river. They hide under the rocks, but some drift in the current at dawn and dusk every day. The trout recognize them.

An important point to consider in fishing Salmon Fly nymphs is their diversity of size. Consider that after this year's crop of nymphs have emerged, the next generation that will hatch as nymphs about a year later will be considerably smaller. For example, I like to use size-4 and -6 nymphs early in the season, just prior to the Salmon Fly hatch. After it is over you need to drop down a couple of sizes to more realistically match the size of the naturals still in the river.

FISHING DRY FLIES

Dry-fly fishing involves a lot of casting and covering the water, because you usually don't see many fish actually taking flies from the surface. Concentrate on three pattern styles—a low floating pattern, such as a Bird's Stonefly or Henry's Fork Salmon Fly, a high floating pattern like a Kaufmann's Stimulator or Improved Sofa Pillow, and another pattern, one of the modern foam-bodied flies, that you can skitter on the surface without pulling it under. Another good fly which you can work with plenty of action is the Turck's Tarantula. The clipped deer head, highly visible calf-tail wing, and rubber legs make it ideal for casting near the bank and twitching across the surface to entice strikes.

Why do you need three pattern styles? These huge insects are pretty clumsy fliers when they take to the air. Many of them go crashing to the surface; others fall out of the bushes and land on the water. They usually flutter along or skate, trying to swim back to the bank using their legs as paddles. The trout really get excited when they see that and if you can't impart a similar action to your pattern, it will likely go unnoticed.

After lots of naturals have been on the water for awhile, usually later in the afternoon, they drift along listlessly in the current for hundreds of yards. The trout will then take up holding positions and sip the big morsels without much disturbance to the water's surface. The problem is, these low floaters are often very hard to see.

High floaters will drift in the fast runs while still offering good visibility to both the angler and the trout. Sometimes a fly tied with some white or orange in the wing will help with the visibility problem. After all, if you can't see your fly you won't know if you are getting the proper drift and more importantly, you may miss a strike if a big head just slips up through the heavy current and inhales your fly.

In addition to the standard dry-fly and nymph tactics for Salmon Flies, there is one really effective tactic that is rarely ever used these days. That is to fish a Salmon Fly pattern wet, just under the surface. This is the way I grew up fishing the Salmon Fly hatch. I used to go up and fish Box Canyon all the time and fish with a pattern called the Triple Bar X, an old Montana pattern with a woven-hair body and a squirrel-tail wing. It probably accounted for more fish than we catch now with the dry flies that we use.

We didn't use waders back then and we would just wade wet down the river in our jeans and Converse All-Stars, casting toward the bank and teasing the fly along. We didn't use backing so when we would hook a big trout, we just went right down the river chasing it, bouncing off rocks and treading water if it was too deep to wade. I usually came home with some pretty good bruises on my legs, but at least I could land the big trout by staying close to them as they charged down the fast currents.

To my knowledge, nobody ties the Triple Bar X anymore, but you can make this work with the patterns already in your box. Just trim down one of your dry fly patterns. I like to take a Bird's Stone, trim some of the wing and some of the hackle and just fish it wet.

You can cast it out and across and let it slowly swing in the current, as if you were fishing for steelhead. I like a double-fly rig with the larger Salmon Fly imitation as the top fly and a smaller Woolly Bugger or soft hackle wet fly for the bottom pattern. Another good method is to just drop a wet fly off the back of a high-floating dry fly like a foam-bodied Salmon Fly or a Turck's Tarantula.

Like many other western rivers, there are other hatches which coincide with the Salmon Fly hatch on the Henry's Fork. There are usually some good hatches of caddisflies, especially the Great Gray Spotted Sedge (*Arctopsyche grandis*), and smaller Golden Stoneflies. Often the water is a little too high and the current too fast for big trout to hold and feed on the caddisflies. So most of the caddis fishing will be in little pockets next to the bank where fish can find some shelter. When you're floating, you'll likely drift by good holding water and cast a Salmon Fly imitation in there and the fish won't take it because they're keyed in on the caddisflies. If you're fishing dries, it's not a bad idea to fish two flies, one a Salmon Fly, the other a caddisfly. You can also use the same technique with nymphs with a big black nymph as the top fly and a caddis larva as a dropper.

Maybe the most important concurrent hatch during this time is the Golden Stone hatch. Year in and year out, it is more reliable that the Salmon Fly hatch. Use the same type of patterns you need for the larger Salmon Flies except a couple of sizes smaller. The naturals are also much lighter and more of a golden amber in color. I normally use size-8 and -10 Golden Stone patterns. Again, a double-fly rig is great with a Salmon Fly and Golden Stone combo.

A few years ago I was floating the lower Henry's Fork with my two sons, Shaun and Chris, during the Salmon Fly hatch and the river was unusually crowded. It had been a very late spring after a hard winter with heavy snowpack. All of the other rivers in the region were completely blown out, so there were drift boats from eight states. I wasn't very optimistic because there were boats going down both banks less than a hundred yards apart. The trout probably knew more about all of the different Salmon Fly patterns than the fly shop proprietors.

We tried all kinds of different patterns and techniques but the trout didn't seem to show much interest. Then I saw a couple of Golden Stones mixed in with some Salmon Flies on a tree next to the bank. I reasoned that all the other anglers were probably fishing big Salmon Fly patterns. I tied on a size-10 Henry's Fork Golden Stone and immediately started catching trout.

Another idea that came to mind was that everyone seemed to be fishing out of the boat. There weren't many anglers trying to wade and fight the heavy current. We pulled the boat in along some large rocks, ate some lunch, and rested. Looking upstream we realized there was a lot of holding water that couldn't be covered properly by casting from the boats. We worked upstream, covering all of the water as we went.

There were a couple of large rocks just under the surface about ten feet from the bank. This made it impossible to get a natural drift from a boat. I made a good cast just between the rocks and the bank and hooked two nice rainbows. Another cast at the top of the inside rock produced a solid, heavy take. The fish bored down through the fast current and I had to chase him downstream. After a tough fight I finally landed a beautiful brown that would have easily topped five pounds.

There was no way you could have gotten a good drift over that fish from a boat. The only way was to cast upstream, inside the big rocks. The Golden Stone pattern probably helped fool that brown. He had probably seen dozens of big Salmon Fly patterns dragged over him all morning. He gained the confidence to take my fly because he saw a smaller fly, different from all the other patterns he had seen, drifting over his lie.

CHAPTER 4

Caddisflies

*T*here are probably few rivers as famous for mayfly hatches as the Henry's Fork. There is good reason for that. There are twelve major mayfly species which emerge throughout the season, not to mention all of the minor hatches. But there are times of the year when the caddisflies are even more important than the mayflies. I haven't found it to be essential to know all the species of caddisflies in the river; I look at it like there's a papa caddis, a momma caddis, and a baby caddis. I look at sizes and colors. Caddisflies tend to be generic. They all have pretty drab colors and come in a range of sizes. You can carry a selection of flies and be ready for the hatches on this river.

We are fortunate on the Henry's Fork. On many rivers the caddisfly community is still a mystery. Here we have a complete and accurate listing for the full fishing season of all the major hatches. When Gary LaFontaine was gathering specimens for his book, *Caddisflies*, he spent three summers on the Henry's Fork. One of his collection sites (there were ten of them on the river) was the back window of my shop. His

72

samples were identified by Dr. Oliver Flint of the Smithsonian Institution. So we know where, when, and how the major species of caddisflies hatch up and down the river. With this information you can be at the right spot with the right fly when a particular species is going to emerge or lay eggs.

For the beginner, it's really much more important to understand the biology of the caddisfly. They are very closely related to butterflies and moths. Their life cycle consists of egg, larva, pupa, and adult phases. The eggs are laid underwater where they hatch into larvae. The larvae are wormlike in appearance; some roam free, some build nets but no cases, and others build cases. The pupa is the stage in which the larva closes off the case (or builds a case) and goes through a period of metamorphosis. The adult emerges by escaping the thin sheath of the pupa at the surface. Unlike mayflies, the adults can take flight immediately because they don't need to ride on the surface to dry their wings. That's why big trout don't normally waste their energy trying to eat the adults. Experience teaches them that the pupa, half in and half out of the surface film, offers a much easier catch.

To properly cover the caddis hatches, you need patterns to imitate the larva, emerging pupa, adult, and egg-laying adult. It isn't as simple as with mayflies. There are two different types of larvae, some with cases and some without cases. Some adults emerge under the water and swim to the surface to emerge while others pop out on the surface. Some egg-layers fall on the water like mayfly spinners while others dive under the water to lay their eggs. Learn to observe the naturals on the stream. Caddis can be very complicated if you let them. Learn to keep it simple.

The larvae can be divided into cased caddis that build little houses around their bodies from weeds, rocks, or sticks; net-builders that make little nets like tiny spider webs to filter their food; and free-roaming larvae that roam about the streambed searching for food. There are patterns to imitate each type. The Cased Caddis Larva and the Peeking Caddis are tied with dark rough material to represent the case with a green or cream head to represent the larva "peeking" out of the case. Believe it or not, these types of patterns are very effective when fished deep in the runs. The net-builders and free-roaming larvae look pretty much the same. Patterns like the Serendipity and Free-Living Caddis Larva work well to imitate them.

When the caddis are actually emerging, LaFontaine's Sparkle Pupa, both the Deep Emergent versions, are pretty hard to beat. These were the first flies tied with Antron, the bright, flat-sided nylon fiber. Of the two patterns, the Emergent Sparkle Pupa is my favorite. I like it better because I grease it and fish it right in the surface film, just like a dry fly. My biggest concern with the LaFontaine patterns is that the commercial versions are often over-dressed. They should be tied sparsely, especially if you're fishing them on flat, clear water.

Two colors are indispensable because they match the two main caddis colors. A bright olive green, and a dark tan, sort of an amber. I also have had a lot of success with a Partridge Caddis Emerger, which is a modification of the LaFontaine pattern, tied in the same color schemes.

Finally, there two classic patterns that stand out as caddis-fly imitations. The Gold-Ribbed Hare's Ear Nymph was undoubtedly tied to imitate a mayfly nymph with a tapered body and a dark wing case pulled over a robust thorax. I think it works better as a caddis larva imitation because it looks rough and rugged, just like a cased caddis larva. Another of my all-time favorite flies is the Renegade. You can fish it wet or dry. I know it doesn't look much like a caddisfly, but with the peacock body and brown and cream fore-and-aft hackle, it has always been a dynamite pattern for me during caddisfly hatches.

The type of water you fish will dictate the fly you use to imitate the adult. Caddisflies are important in all types of water. If you're fishing fast water you need patterns that offer good visibility. For rough water the two patterns I like the best are the Elk Hair Caddis, created by my friend Al Troth, and an offshoot of it called a Peacock Caddis. The latter is much darker, with a peacock body and a dark deer-hair wing.

One of the best materials I've found when developing patterns for slow, spring-creek water is the breast feathers from gray partridge or from other game birds like grouse and quail. These feathers hold their shape, even when wet, and they provide a realistic profile of the wing. The Spent Partridge Caddis is a pattern I developed many years ago to imitate the egg-laying caddis on the slow waters of the Henry's Fork. It was originally tied to lay flat in the film to imitate the egg-layers, but I also tie it with a full hackle so it sits higher on the water. In more recent years, as my vision has started to dull, I've included a parachute postwing for better visibility. I call it the E-Z Caddis because it is easier for me to see.

Another great pattern to imitate many of the adult caddisflies on the Henry's Fork is the Hemingway Special. Many years ago my wife and I tied flies commercially for Cal Gates' shop in Grayling, Michigan. Cal had us tie several variations of the Henryville Special to imitate specific Au Sable River caddisflies. I tried another variation for the Henry's Fork with medium or dark dun hackle. My friend, Jack Hemingway, especially liked them, so instead of naming the new fly the Henry's Fork Caddis, we decided to call it the Hemingway Special.

The female caddisflies that lay their eggs underwater create a special problem. They carry a cluster of air bubbles down with them, giving themselves a silvery overcoat. No ordinary fly matches this bright look. A Diving Caddis wet fly, with a body of Antron yarn and an overwing of clear Antron fibers, can be really effective. The old style of fishing two or even three wet flies at once, casting them across stream and mending, works spectacularly. Right at dark, when it is impossible to see anymore, this is the way to cover the water on the lower river.

Some of the best caddis fishing on the Henry's Fork occurs in April and May. Unfortunately, only a small portion of the Henry's Fork is open to fishing at this time of year. Most of the river doesn't open until Memorial Day weekend, but the stretch between Ashton and St. Anthony has some outstanding caddis hatches early in the season. The American Grannom, locally known as the "Mother's Day Hatch," has a green body and a fairly dark mottled wing. The common size is 14. My favorite way to fish this hatch is to use a dark dry fly like a Hemingway Caddis or dark Elk Hair Caddis and tie on a bright green Caddis Emerger as a dropper. My favorite pattern is a Partridge Emerger but I also like LaFontaine's Emergent Sparkle Pupa.

This hatch produces some incredible fishing on the lower Henry's Fork until the water gets too high and dirty in mid-May from spring runoff. The hatch is usually still going on when the larger stoneflies start to emerge in late May. You can also find them at Last Chance when the general fishing season opens. In my opinion, the American Grannom is one of the most important caddis hatches on the Henry's Fork, second only to the Spotted Sedge (*Hydropsyche occidentalis* and *H. cockerelli*).

Another strong surge of the American Grannom (a slightly different species) comes off during the middle of the summer, in late July and August. Insects cloud the sky in the evening and produce some exceptional dry-fly fishing in the mornings from Last Chance to Riverside Campground below Osborne Bridge.

By mid-June the caddis are really going throughout the entire Henry's Fork system. The Long-Horn Sedge (*Oecetis disjuncta* and *O. avara*), Spotted Sedge, Little Sister Sedge (*Cheumatopsyche campyla*), and Green Sedge (*Rhyacophila bifida*) all make their presence known in a big way. If you're not sure what pattern to use, try to catch a couple of the naturals and check out the wing and body color. Then it's just a matter of selecting a pattern in the proper size and color.

It is common for several species of caddisflies to be all mixed together. Another complicating factor is that the adults of one species might be emerging while the egg-layers of another species are landing on the surface or diving underwater to lay their eggs. This can drive anyone crazy. Sometimes caddis fishing is impossible; sometimes it's easy. In fact, one guy will be trying to catch trout on his "ole reliable," while another guy is crawling along the bank with his insect net trying to figure out what is going on. Have you ever tried to catch an adult caddis? Both types of anglers are having fun.

You won't go wrong if you use a slow-water pattern like a Hemingway Special or Spent Partridge Caddis. In my experience, hair-winged caddis patterns don't work as well on the slow-water areas of the Henry's Fork. I also like a sparse Caddis Emerger with a rough Antron body, trailing shuck, and a partridge wing with a peacock collar. It is a killer when used as a dropper with one of the dry-fly patterns. The best color in June is green; later on I like tan.

One of the most perplexing hatches of the entire season is the tiny microcaddis, commonly known as the Weedy Water Sedge (*Amiocentrus aspilus*). While it is certainly one of the most important hatches on the river, it also may be the most challenging. The fish almost always get hyperselective on those little flies. These will be the typical bank feeders in the late afternoon. But it's still extremely difficult to get the fish to take.

In June and September, fish will concentrate on Weedy Water Sedges behind weed bunkers on the Railroad Ranch section. (Photo by Barry and Cathy Beck)

Ernie Schwiebert once told me that he heard a guy cursing up a blue streak late one afternoon. Then he saw the guy hurl his beautiful cane rod into the river. As the guy stomped up the bank Ernie asked him about the rod. "To hell with it," the guy exclaimed! "I've had enough of this to last me a life time!" The guy never came back to hunt for the rod. Another casualty of the Weedy Water Sedge.

The only pattern I've found that works consistently is a very dark Spent Partridge Caddis tied on a size-22 hook. You may need to clip it down so it rides flush in the surface film. Work in close to a feeding trout so you can see your fly. It usually takes many accurate casts to get enough drifts over the feeding fish. If you sense your frustration is starting to turn to outrage, head down to the A-Bar, only a few hundred yards upriver. You might have a hangover in the morning but you'll save on your fly fishing equipment.

The larvae of the Weedy Water Sedge concentrate in the river in big, billowing beds of weeds (*Ranunculus*). These

White Wyethia blooms in moist meadows about the same time as the Green Drake emerges in June. (Photo by Stan Bradshaw)

sedges peak in late June and again in September. To fish them during the emergence, get right behind the weed bunkers where the fish stack up. Fish them during the evening spinner fall, when the females come back to lay their eggs on the surface. The fish just sip these tiny caddisflies. Often anglers expect fish rising to caddis to make a lot of disturbance on the surface, but it doesn't happen when taking these little micro caddis because they are the equivalent of mayfly spinners, lying on the water crumpled and dying.

Don't forget that caddisflies hatch in both the evenings and the mornings. When you look for caddisfly hatches in the evenings, remember that they will be hatching again in the morning during the mayfly hatches.

The Little Sister Sedge (*Cheumatopsyche campyla*) hatches in massive numbers throughout warm nights in midsummer. In the mornings the water is still littered with the bodies of this size-16 tan insect, and trout will sip a small dry fly drifting against the bank. Sometimes, they feed so selectively on the left over cripples that they ignore the newly hatching morning mayflies. This can be one of those puzzling masking hatches.

During the summer at dawn, you will also find the Black Dancer (*Mystacides alafimbriata*), a tremendously prolific insect on the Henry's Fork. It's a slow-water caddisfly, not important on most trout streams, but important on the Henry's Fork. In August, right before dark, masses of these caddisflies come off in the Bonefish Flats area of Harriman Park. One pattern that matches it well is a dark gray, almost black, Hemingway Special. You can also use a dark Partridge Caddis, tied with the dark dun body feathers of a California quail. If you hunt these cute little game birds, save the feathers. Both of these flies are fairly delicate flat-water imitations.

The Long-Horn Sedges are always around in late summer. Often this is when there is a lot of grass and weed floating in the water on the Ranch Section of the river. You can have this piece of the Henry's Fork all to yourself because no one wants to pick goop off their hook after every cast. And yet the trout will rise in between the pieces of grass and weed. Try using an upside down fly, a Dancing Caddis, which matches the Long-Horn Sedge. Use a knotless leader. Make short casts and keep your rod high. This is exciting dry-fly fishing.

The good caddisfly hatches continue until mid-September in the Harriman Park, or Ranch, section of the Henry's Fork. Don't make the mistake of believing the Henry's Fork is only a mayfly stream. You don't want to get caught without your caddis imitations. In some ways, caddisflies may be even more important than mayflies on the Henry's Fork.

CHAPTER 5

Mayflies

*T*he big three mayfly hatches on western spring creeks are the Blue-Winged Olive (*Baetis*), Pale Morning Dun (*Ephemerella inermis*), and Trico (*Tricorythodes minutus*). Water temperature, water type, and water quality are the limiting factors. Some streams have year-round average temperatures that are too cold for Tricos and PMD's and only support Blue-Winged Olives because they can complete their life cycle in colder water. Some of the top western trout streams, like the Big Horn and Missouri Rivers in Montana, support all three of these mayfly species.

Probably no other trout river in this country, or the rest of the world for that matter, has the diversity and density of mayfly species. On the Henry's Fork at least twelve major mayfly species appear in significant numbers, including the big three.

BLUE-WINGED OLIVE
Three distinct species commonly called Blue-Winged Olives (BWOs) occur on the Henry's Fork and make up the

first major mayfly hatch of the season. Two of the species have been reclassified—one that was not a *Baetis* is now classified as a *Baetis*, and another that was a *Baetis* and now is not. From the fly fisher's point of view, they are all Blue-Winged Olives.

All three *Baetis* species that occur on the Henry's Fork are multibrooded, which means that they emerge more than one time a year, mainly spring and fall. *Baetis tricaudatus* kicks off the season in March and also emerges from mid-September until early November.

Diphetor hageni was known as *Baetis parvus* until it got reclassified. Fortunately for us, even though the rainbows in the Harriman State Park are often referred to as "having their PhDs," most of them don't know Latin, let alone when a mayfly on their menu gets reclassified. The third Blue-Winged Olive is *Baetis punctiventris*, previously known as *Pseudocloeon edmundsi*. These two species of Blue-Winged Olives emerge in June and again in September. They are much more important in September when there aren't many larger mayflies to choose from.

You need imitations of the dun and the emerger to properly fish the Blue-Winged Olive hatches. I like no-hackles and thorax patterns. CDC emerger patterns also are very effective. All of the *Baetis* are similar in color with a grayish olive body. *Baetis tricaudatus* and *Diphetor hageni* have dark gray wings, while *Baetis punctiventris* has a light wing. I honestly don't think the trout care.

The early season *Baetis* is a bit larger than the other two. You can sometimes get by with a pattern as large as size 16. The September Blue-Winged Olives are tiny. Size 20 and 22 will match them just about right.

Characteristic of *Baetis*, the spinners don't swarm, mate, and die on the surface like most other mayflies. Instead, the duns concentrate at streamside and, after molting and mating, crawl under the water to lay their eggs. There is evidence that the males, as well as the females, crawl into the water. When you think of the harsh conditions these small mayflies must encounter, it is easy to understand nature's way of helping them survive to propagate their species. The underwater egg-layers can be matched with a Diving Blue-Winged Olive Egg Layer, a fly with a wing of clear Antron. It is effective fished as a dropper below a dry fly.

As a general rule, the timing of the spinner fall depends upon the timing of the dun's emergence. If the emergence comes off in the morning, the spinner fall occurs the same evening. If the duns emerge in the afternoon, the spinner fall comes the next morning. The one exception to this is that the spinner fall of the *Baetis tricaudatus* comes shortly after the hatch in the afternoon.

WESTERN MARCH BROWN

The other early-season mayfly hatch is the Western March Brown, sometimes referred to as a Black Quill. The species is *Rithrogena morrisoni*. It belongs to a family of mayflies that emerge just under the surface, so a wet-fly emerger is extremely effective. These large mayflies emerge throughout the month of May and are frequently seen when the Harriman Park opens to fishing on June 15.

They often hatch with the smaller Blue-Winged Olives and it sometimes seems that the trout are not really interested in these large, dark mayflies. During emergence the nymphs cling to the bottom then, after breaking out of the nymphal shuck, the freshly emerged duns float to the surface. The subsurface emergers offer such tempting morsels that the trout sometimes completely ignore the dun after they reach the surface.

My favorite pattern is a size-12 Soft Hackle with a pheasant tail or hare's ear body. The trout will hold in the slots where they can pick off the emerging duns. You may need a small split shot to get the fly down. Sometimes I like to use a two-fly rig with the emerger trailing a dark buoyant dry fly. My favorite dry fly is a dark Quill Gordon in size 14.

While the Western March Browns prefer faster water, you will find them dispersed throughout the Henry's Fork. Above St. Anthony they provide some fantastic fishing in May along with the caddis hatches, and they generate some of the best dry-fly fishing at Last Chance when the Idaho general season opens that continues until mid-June.

PALE MORNING DUN

The Pale Morning Dun (PMD) is the crank that turns the wheel on the mayfly hatches of the Henry's Fork. It is hard to imagine any spring creek without a large number of these yellowish mayflies riding the soft currents and lifting into the morning air. Distributed throughout the Henry's Fork drainage, they are as important on the tailwater from Ashton to St. Anthony as they are through Harriman State Park. The upper reaches of the river also support a good population.

The Pale Morning Duns start to hatch in June and actually continue almost through the summer, well into August. Color can be important when you're matching the PMD, but it can also be confusing. These flies are similar to their close cousins, the Hendricksons, common to Midwestern and Eastern waters. The PMD males are sometimes darker and more brownish than the females.

Occasionally anglers come into the shop thinking they've discovered a new species. They show me a sample that has a red-brown mahogany body and a dark wing. When I tell them it is a Pale Morning Dun they look at me like I have ten heads.

Pale Morning Duns also show slight differences in coloration according to the watershed. They appear to be much brighter and more chartreuse on the spring creeks of the Paradise Valley near Livingston, Montana. On the South Fork of the Snake, the Pale Morning Duns are more pinkish in coloration. In fact, there are guides there who swear the fish won't take anything except a Pink Cahill Parachute. On the Henry's Fork the color is a more subdued chartreuse with a grayish cast.

The color variations of the PMDs have even misled some of the best angling entomologists. Doug Swisher and Carl Richards, in *Selective Trout*, identified three different species of PMDs on the Henry's Fork. I've collected hundreds of samples at different times of the year and on different stretches of the Henry's Fork and sent them to Dr. George Edmunds, noted aquatic entomologist at the University of Utah. All of them were identified as *Ephemerella inermis*.

More important than color is the stage of the hatch. You need patterns to imitate the nymph, emerger, dun, and spinner. Since these mayflies continue to hatch through the heat of the summer, you will also need some good cripple patterns because lots of duns never fully escape the nymphal shuck. The size will vary from size 16 in June to size 20 in August.

Early in the season when the weather is cool, the fish key on the duns, and you want a No-Hackle or a Thorax pattern. But in late summer, when the weather gets hot, things really change. Few of the duns stay on the water very long, so the fish focus on patterns in the surface film and just below.

The daily cycle on the Pale Morning Dun is as follows: Spinner fall starts about 9:30 a.m., duns begin at about 11:00 a.m. and go all afternoon, and then about 8:00 p.m. the spinners start up again. Weather conditions may affect this daily cycle. If it's cool and cloudy, you'll get the concentrated hatch in the middle part of the morning. If the weather is warm and dry, these little flies will hatch sporadically throughout the day. You won't see a good concentration on the water because the duns escape and immediately fly off the water. During mid-July and August, you'll see trout boiling in the surface yet you can't see anything on the water. Look in the air and you'll likely see dozens of PMDs taking flight that have emerged from the surface. The trout really get into the emerging duns and cripples. They can be some of the most selective trout you'll ever encounter.

A couple of years ago I went with a good friend, Dom Traverso, to try to "tame the lions" down on Wood Road #16. Dom is one of the best spring creek anglers I know and he has developed some very effective patterns to use for these toughest of trout.

There were trout rising everywhere, sporadically boiling the surface for the emerging duns as they wiggled and twisted to escape their nymphal shucks. We split up, about 200 feet apart, and spent the next three hours without changing position. The trout moved upstream as they fed and when the first one was past, another would soon follow. I was on my knees, to lower my profile and to help me see the fly better. I'm sure Dom thought I was kneeling to ask for celestial guidance.

I used a Half Back Emerger, a pattern I developed that incorporates deer hair pulled over the back of the fly, kind of like a Humpy. I hooked and landed a couple of very nice trout and Dom did the same. As we walked back to the truck we felt the fishing gods had richly blessed us. Those lions can really eat you alive and we had both managed to tame a couple of them. The Pale Morning Dun hatch can be like that.

TRICO

The common name for this tiny, robust mayfly is an abbreviation for its Latin name, *Tricorythodes*. The nymphs prefer soft bottom silt and weed beds in the slower sections of the Henry's Fork. They are distributed throughout the Harriman Park, from Last Chance to Pinehaven. I have not found Tricos to be significant on other sections of the river.

The Trico spinner fall happens later on the Henry's Fork than on other regional spring creeks and rivers. It doesn't really get going until about August 20. The Trico is a small fly, so imitate it with size 20 or smaller patterns.

The duns hatch early in the mornings and late in the evenings right up until dark. The spinners, the best known phase of the Trico, fall on the water right after the duns hatch. In fact, these sex-crazed mayflies really get with it. They take to the air, molt in the air, mate and come back to the water within an hour or two. As with other insects, however, the timing of when to fish will depend on how warm the weather is. As you get into late September, the Tricos don't get on the water until almost noon.

The feeding behavior of the trout on Tricos is distinctive. Big rainbows pack into little pods where there'll be several big fish all together; the pod looks like a little riffle. As you look downstream, you can see this disturbance in the water. And it's always big fish that are slurping these Trico spinners.

As important as the spinner fall is, the duns can be equally important early in the morning. I like two different patterns to imitate the duns; a size-20 to -22 no-hackle with white wings and black body or a parachute in the same size and color combination. While the body of a Trico is normally imitated with black, they are actually olive in appearance. Like many other mayflies, the male has a dark body and the female has a pale chalk-olive abdomen. The thorax of both the male and female is very dark, almost black.

Henry's Fork fish also feed heavily on the Trico nymphs. It's hard to get people to use a size-20 nymph but it can be really effective and not all that difficult to fish. If you grease the leader right down to the nymph, the nymph will sit in the surface film, and you will see the fish rise when it takes the nymph. Another good way to fish a small nymph is to use it as a dropper off a parachute dry fly. I just run the tippet through the eye of the dry fly and then tie another piece of tippet with a clinch knot below the top fly, allowing it to slide freely on the tippet. The clinch knot is big enough in diameter to keep it from sliding down to the bottom fly.

The spinners are the most difficult stage of the Trico to fish because there are so many of them on the water that it can be tough to see your fly. You need to get close to the fish and time your casts to coincide with the trout's feeding pattern. You don't always need to use a spent-wing pattern which rides flush in the surface. I've had great success using a parachute pattern. I've also found a tiny Royal Wulff to be a great asset when fishing the Trico spinners. It is easy for me to see and for the trout to notice. Sometimes the spinners clump together and a size-18 or -20 Renegade will get the trouts' attention.

WESTERN GREEN DRAKE

We call it a "Western" Green Drake because there is also a Green Drake that hatches in the East that belongs to a different family of mayflies. Our Green Drake is actually a very close cousin to the smaller Pale Morning Dun. The Green Drake is classified as *Drunella grandis*. It is a large, robust mayfly about 16 millimeters in length; tie it on a size-10 hook.

The Green Drake hatch is best known on the Railroad Ranch, but it is also very important on the lower river and the section above the Island Park Reservoir.

The fish really get after the Green Drakes but I think it's important to realize that they don't rush out and start feeding on them as soon as the first duns come out. The first couple of days you'll find the little fish coming up and slashing at these Drakes. It takes the large fish two or three days to key on the Green Drakes.

The emergence dates vary from year to year. I've seen them start as early as June 10 at Last Chance. The latest I can remember was July 1. A lot depends on the kind of spring weather and stream flow regime. There were some drought years where the river ran fairly low with warm weather in the spring which caused the drakes to hatch earlier than normal, at times as much as a week to ten days. In general, the best fishing for the Green Drake hatch is from June 20 until around the second week of July.

Weather can really affect the hatch. If it's hot and warm when the hatch is coming out, the flies will hatch sporadically. The best day you could have would be cold, cloudy, and drizzly.

You should have four patterns for the Green Drake hatch—a nymph, an emerger, a dun, and a spinner. The nymphs are plump and robust. A dark Gold-Ribbed Hare's Ear is a good match but I also tie a more exact imitation with dark gray and olive dubbing and mottled partridge for legs. Fishing the nymph can be very productive in the morning before the hatch comes off.

It takes these big mayflies some time to break out of their nymphal shucks, dry their wings, and get airborne. For that reason, fishing emergers and cripples is productive. During the dun emergence, the insects are quite bright, so I want a bright green fly. I use a lot of bright yellow intermixed in the olive to achieve this brightness. I like a soft hackle emerger with a bright olive body and bright chartreuse hackle. If I only had one pattern to use for the Green Drake hatch it would be a cripple with a trailing shuck protruding through the surface film (Green Drake Cripple). I tie the shuck of marabou blended with a few fibers of Z-Lon. The dark elk-hair wing extends forward over the eye with a parachute hackle.

One of the most popular patterns is the Paradrake. The Paradrake has a dark postwing and an extended body of dark olive elk hair ribbed with bright yellow thread. The bright chartreuse hackle is wrapped parachute-style on the wing. The body should extend no more than the width of the hook gap or you'll start missing a lot of strikes. If you tie the Paradrake, you should use a small hook. It's the body size you you want to duplicate, not the hook size.

A Wulff-style dry fly can also work well. Use dark elk for the wings, chartreuse hackle, moose hair for the tail, and an olive body ribbed with yellow floss.

For many years we erroneously assumed that the spinners were not important. When they are on the water you need to have a big pattern to match them. I like a size-10 spent spinner with speckled gray partridge hackle tips and a dark olive-brown body ribbed with yellow floss. On warm days the spinners come early. I've seen them on the water at 7:00 a.m.

One day I was fishing a favorite run just below the middle bridge in the Railroad Ranch during the Green Drake hatch when Pat Barnes came drifting by in his wooden drift boat with "Ole Pro" lettered on the bow. Pat was a great friend who bought Green Drakes from us when my wife and I first started tying flies commercially. Pat was also a big help when I first started guiding on his home river, the Madison. He had his Lab with him and seemed to be having a great time.

He pulled in and asked me if I wanted to float the rest of the way out. I got on the oars and had one of the most memorable fishing days of my life. Pat whooped and cheered every time one of those big rainbows came up and smashed his Green Drake. The twinkle in his eye when he released a fish was a testimony to what fly fishing is all about. Pat Barnes was a class act. I doubt I would ever have had the success I've enjoyed in the fly-fishing business without examples like Jim Danskin, Bud Lilly, Dan Bailey, and the "Ole Pro" himself. I frequently sit on the rock where he picked me up and reminisce.

BROWN DRAKE

The Green Drake isn't the only big mayfly that hatches on the Henry's Fork. The Brown Drake (*Ephemerella simulans*) is a little longer than the Green Drake but not quite as robust. The nymph is a burrower, so you find it in the slower reaches of the Henry's Fork where the silt is concentrated. There are no Brown Drakes on the Henry's Fork below Ashton but you can find good numbers in three locations: the slower water of Harriman State Park, the slower water above Coffee Pot rapids upstream from Island Park Reservoir, and Buffalo River (the tributary).

The timing of this hatch coincides with the Green Drake hatch, from around June 20 until early July. The Brown Drakes normally stick around a week or so later than the Green Drakes. You usually don't find both species in the same water because they prefer different habitats. The Brown Drake emerges in the late evening. It will start hatching around seven or eight o'clock at night. At that time of year you have daylight until almost 10 p.m.

All three stages of the Brown Drake hatch—the emerging nymph, the dun, and the spinner—are equally important, and they all happen at the same time. One fish may be taking nymphs and the next fish may be sipping the duns, and a third may be hitting the spinner.

Fishing the nymphs can be quite productive. As emergence approaches they abandon the safety of their burrows and, after scurrying across the stream bottom, they begin a rapid ascent to toward the surface. Just below the surface the emerging duns break free of their nymphal casings and float gently to the top. The trout really load up on the fast swimming nymphs and emergers.

The nymph, simply called a Brown Drake Nymph, should be tied on a long-shank hook with pale yellowish tan dubbing and brown mottled partridge for legs. I also tie in some gray ostrich herl or philo plume for gills. Use a nymph when you see fish bulging or ripping wakes under the surface. Cast above such a fish and retrieve with a fast twitch.

Like the nymph, the emerger (a Brown Drake Soft Hackle Emerger) should also be tied with rough yellowish tan dubbing. I like long soft hackle fibers of grouse or partridge and a swept-back wing of partridge hackle tips. You can twitch the emerger or fish it dead drift, just under the surface.

As it is for the Green Drake, the Paradrake is a great imitation of the dun. Use light tan elk for the body ribbed with brown thread, a dark brown elk hair postwing with ginger hackle. Another good pattern to imitate the dun is tied with a reversed wood duck flank feather for the extended abdomen, yellowish tan dubbing for the thorax, and an upright wing of brown partridge or mottled hen hackle tips. The ginger hackle should be tied thorax style.

The big spinners normally hit the water around dark. They frequently drift along on the current with their wings upright while others will rest with their wings in the traditional spent position. I like the same spent spinner described for the Green Drake in a color scheme to represent the Brown Drake. I like to use hackle on the Brown Drake Spinner, clipped on the bottom to offer better visibility in the late evening hours.

Whitefish can really be a problem when fishing the Brown Drakes. They seem to go crazy over these large insects.

The Gray Drake nymphs crawl out of the river to emerge, attaching themselves to rocks or vegetation while they make the transformation from emerger to dun. (Photo by Mike Lawson)

Even the most experienced anglers have trouble discerning the whitefish from the trout. The only thing you can do is move on if all you are catching are whitefish. If you find a school of big fish rising, chances are they are whitefish.

There are always exceptions. The largest trout I've ever landed in the Railroad Ranch stretch of the river was rising to Brown Drakes right in the middle of a bunch of big whitefish. They were making a lot of disturbance with their loud, splashy rises. I watched them carefully and saw one fish that was questionable. I felt it was a big whitefish, but I couldn't be sure, so I made a cast over it. When I tightened on the fly the water exploded. When the trout vaulted into the air there was no mistake. Boy, was I glad I decided to make that cast. When I finally landed him he measured just under 26 inches in length and he was as fat as a football.

GRAY DRAKE

Probably the least known large mayfly that occurs on the Henry's Fork is the Gray Drake, yet it may be the most important. The species is *Siphlonurus occidentalis* (sounds like a bad disease you can catch from too much fishing). The nymphs are classified as swimmers, which means they roam freely, moving into the sloughs, ponds, stream margins, and other slack-water areas. They can migrate miles from the main river over the course of their one-year life span. Fortunately they can dart quickly enough to escape from predators.

One feature unique to the Gray Drake is that the nymphs crawl out to emerge. Like stoneflies, they attach themselves to vegetation, rocks, or other structure so the transformation from nymph to dun takes place out of the water. Consequently, emergers and duns are not usually important food sources for fish (or objects of angler imitation).

Since the duns, emergers, and even nymphs are of minor importance, the only stage anglers need to worry about is the spinner. After the duns molt, the spinners concentrate over riffles where they mate and lay their eggs. While the types of spinner imitations I described for the other large drakes are effective, you usually don't need to get too sophisticated. These mayflies often are so thick on the water that having a highly visible fly is of the utmost importance. My favorite is a size-10 Parachute Adams.

There are Gray Drakes throughout the Yellowstone region but there are probably no concentrations comparable to those found on the Henry's Fork from the Ashton Dam down to the confluence with the South Fork, although I've also had some exceptional fishing on the lower reaches of Fall River.

The Henry's Fork below Ashton Dam has incredible hatches of Gray Drakes. (Photo by Mike Lawson)

This exceptional spinner fall coincides with the Green Drake and Brown Drake hatches up in the Railroad Ranch. It is possible to fish the Green Drake hatch at Last Chance in the morning and catch the Gray Drakes in the afternoon near St. Anthony. The spinners start to swarm about 2 p.m. and hit the water soon thereafter. One of the greatest obstacles to fishing the Gray Drake hatch is wind. Wind doesn't normally have an effect on emerging mayflies, so they'll still be on the water even if the breeze is so stout you can't cast. Spinners need calm weather to perform their mating dance. If it is too windy, you won't see many spinners.

FLAV

Like the Trico, the common name for this mayfly is synonymous with its Latin classification, *Drunella flavilinea*. It is also known as the Small Western Green Drake (it's about a size 14), partly because it looks almost exactly the same as its closest cousin, the Green Drake. It also shows up in the same kind of water as the Green Drake, but it normally emerges in the afternoon instead of the morning. This hatch is especially good on the afternoons when you get a little bit of cloud cover.

The Flavs overlap with the Green Drakes and Brown Drakes. They usually start showing up in late June and can continue throughout the month of July. Over the years I have learned to associate the timing of the Flav hatch with the finals of the Wimbledon tennis tournament.

The Flav is my favorite mayfly. While it is not as reliable as some other mayflies, like the Pale Morning Dun (on some warm midsummer days you won't see flavs), when afternoon thunderstorms roll in during July, the river literally explodes with them. They are certainly a favorite of the trout as well. I don't know if trout actually have taste preferences, but if they do, the Flav would be at the top of the menu. It doesn't take many of them on the water to cause a feeding frenzy.

Fish them with exactly the same imitations as I have described for the Green Drake, but a couple sizes smaller. I like size 14 or 16. You don't need an extended body for the dun. I like a slate-olive No-Hackle or a Thorax. Cripples and emergers also work but I find the No-Hackle to be the most productive pattern. The same is true for most of the other mayfly hatches as well.

Flav spinners are also significant. The dark olive body should be tied with spent partridge, hen-hackle tips, or CDC. The spinners fall primarily in the midmorning hours, but are frequently seen at dusk on hot July days.

Frequently you have to deal with pesky afternoon breezes when fishing the Flav hatch. An afternoon breeze in Idaho is anything under forty miles per hour. Don't quit fishing just because the wind comes up—I've had some of my greatest days fishing the Flav hatch during windy afternoons. There are ways of dealing with wind.

First, use the wind to assist your approach. You can usually stalk very close to a feeding trout when the wind riffles the surface.

Second, get in a position where the wind helps instead of hinders you. This doesn't always mean you should cast with the wind directly behind you. In fact, sometimes you want to do just the opposite. The wind normally blows upstream in the afternoon on the Henry's Fork. The major problem created by wind is that it hinders a drag-free float. I frequently find that if I cast into the wind, it helps pile the leader up so I can get a longer drag-free drift. When I cast with the wind, my leader lands on the water completely straight, creating an immediate drag on the fly.

Third, cut back on the length of your leader. You don't need a 12-foot leader when the surface is riffled. Try a 7½–footer and you'll be amazed at the difference. And use a shorter tippet.

If you've got the guts to endure a stiff wind, you can often have the river to yourself. I remember a day when the wind was blowing so hard I couldn't keep my hat on. There were trout slashing at the emerging Flavs everywhere and I was the only one crazy enough to be out on the water. I could see a lot of guys looking out the A-Bar windows and I could only guess what they were thinking while leisurely sipping their beers. Meanwhile, I had one of the best fishing days of my life.

CALLIBAETIS

The common name for this mayfly is the Speckled Spinner but almost every angler I know refers to it by its Latin classification *Callibaetis nigritus*. Like the Gray Drake, the nymph is a swimmer. The *Callibaetis* is primarily a lake species and it is rarely found in moving water. The exceptions are some slow-moving spring creeks with heavy aquatic vegetation, including Silver Creek and the Harriman Park stretch of the Henry's Fork.

The *Callibaetis* accounts for the best dry-fly fishing for gulpers on the Island Park Reservoir. The best activity usually occurs when the spinners fall during the midmorning hours. The trout will really focus on the nymphs, however. Tie a streamlined, slender nymph with prominent gills. I tie my favorite pattern, the *Callibaetis* Swimming Nymph, by twisting a couple of strands of pale olive-gray ostrich herl with the tying thread and wrapping it forward to form the abdomen. Place several fibers of brown partridge over the back of the abdomen and rib it with fine gold wire. The thorax should be tied with Antron blended to match the color of the abdomen. I use pearlescent tinsel for the wing case.

When the spinners get on the water it is hard to beat a size-16 Parachute Adams. There are more intricate patterns which more closely represent the natural but the postwing of the parachute is much easier to see on the glassy surface of the lake. Sometimes I drop the *Callibaetis* nymph about 12 inches off the bend of the dry fly.

The Shroud, called a "dry-fly Woolly Bugger" because of its marabou tail, is great for skittering on the lake or river. That makes the fly easy to see when there are a lot of naturals—easy for both fish and angler.

The *Callibaetis* start appearing in mid-June on the reservoir, about a month earlier than on the river. By late July you can count on *Callibaetis* appearing on the slow-water sections of the Harriman State Park. They like slow-moving water with lots of aquatic vegetation. In the late 1980s the Trumpeter Swans that winter there ate most of the aquatic vegetation in the Ranch. The *Callibaetis* were hard to find after that. Since then the swans have been better managed during the winter months and the aquatic plants have rebounded. So have the *Callibaetis*.

On the river the spinners are much more important than the duns. They come to the water about 10 a.m. They frequently sit upright and drift a considerable distance before they lay in the traditional spent position. So I carry some *Callibaetis* with the wings in the upright position as well as some spent spinners. A slate-tan No-Hackle works very well. Another great pattern is a Thorax with a light creamy gray body, grizzly hackle, and a gray partridge wing. The best spinner has light gray tails, a light creamy gray body with gray partridge hackle tips tied spent in a size 16.

Some of the best *Callibaetis* water lies downstream from the middle bridge in the Ranch section, down past the buildings at the main headquarters and below Osborne Bridge on Highway 20. The Bonefish Flats stretch above the middle bridge is also a great location to find *Callibaetis* spinners. They don't seem to be much of a factor on other stretches of the Henry's Fork.

Mahogany Dun

The Mahogany Dun is the most important hatch of September because it's a relatively large mayfly compared to the smaller Tricos and Blue-Winged Olives that are usually on the water at the same time. Mahogany Duns are widely distributed throughout the Harriman State Park downstream to the Pinehaven subdivision. There are also good numbers in the stretch between Ashton and St. Anthony.

The Latin name for the Mahogany Dun is *Paraleptophlebia bicornuta*. There are actually two other species of this genus that hatch on the Henry's Fork, but they emerge sporadically with the Pale Morning Duns so nobody really notices them.

This is a dark mayfly with a dark gray wing and a dark mahogany brown body. The nymphs, duns, and emergers are all important. Spinners generally aren't significant, but you should be prepared with some size-18 Rusty Spinners just in case.

The nymphs are streamlined and capable swimmers, but they usually just drift with the current when dislodged. They wiggle and twist when they rise toward the surface during emergence. I haven't found anything yet which will out-produce a standard Pheasant Tail Nymph when the Mahogany Duns are coming off. Cast it to a rising fish and twitch it slightly or use it as a dropper from a dry fly.

Emergers and cripples are also effective. I like to use a Half Back Emerger with a pheasant tail shuck. For the cripple I like a trailing shuck of rust-colored marabou mixed with a couple of stands of rust Z-Lon. Use reddish tan dubbing for the thorax with a dark deer hair wing.

A size-18 slate-tan No-Hackle will usually out-produce any other pattern when the duns are on the water. Some people don't like No-Hackles because they are so fragile. In fact, the silhouette of the wing actually improves after the quill segments split up. Duck quill fibers are much stronger than elk hair or deer hair, and they are totally water resistant. There isn't a better, more durable natural wing material known to man. In fact, I once managed to get through three different fishing days with the same fly. Admittedly, I didn't catch many fish but I doubt I could have accomplished that feat with any other pattern. If you just can't bring yourself to fish with a No-Hackle, you'll do fine with a Thorax style, which has a dark gray wing and a dark tan body.

CHAPTER 6

Midges

"Midge" does not refer to just any small fly pattern. Midges are aquatic insects of the order Diptera, meaning "two wings," as the adults have only one pair of wings. Mosquitoes, deer flies, gnats, and craneflies are all Diptera. Not all midges are tiny. There are several lake species which can be accurately imitated on a size-12 hook. Many anglers who visit the Henry's Fork probably don't believe these tiny aquatic insects are important because they don't see many of them. That's because midges don't show up in significant numbers until cold weather sets in. Midges account for all of the dry-fly fishing on the Henry's Fork from December through February.

The midge life cycle is similar to that of a caddisfly with egg, larva, pupa, and adult phases. Of all these stages, the pupa is by far the most important to the fly fisher. Midges thrive in cold water and can complete their life cycle in a matter of weeks. Consequently, there will be several generations of midges in a given season.

Midge larvae are wormlike in appearance and are normally at least twice as long as the adult. They come in a
variety of colors with red, olive, and gray being the most
common. Stomach samplings indicate that trout feed heavily on midge larvae. Patterns that produce during the winter
months that have a resemblance to the larvae are the
Brassie in natural copper or red, the Serendipity in red and
olive, and the Variegated Midge Larva with its twist of clear
Antron.

When the larva has matured it pupates. Some forms fas-
ten themselves to bottom structure where they stay until they
emerge. The pupae of Chironomidae, the most common
family that inhabits the Henry's Fork, are free swimming. The
pupa is shorter and more rotund than the skinny larva. The
abdomen is well segmented with a robust thorax composed
of turned-down wing pads, gills, and legs. Because these
pupae are free swimming they can be fished successfully at
any time.

Prior to emergence, the pupae become restless and begin
a series of rises toward the surface, settling back to the bottom between each rise. I have watched this in an aquarium
and it appears the pupae are confused because their protec-
tive sheaths become inflated with gas that buoys them
toward the surface. They seem to fight to stay deep, but eventually, they end up at the surface where they are pinned
against the surface film.

It is easy to see why the trout become very aggressive
when the pupae are rising to the surface in significant numbers. There can be thousands of tiny pupae riding with the
currents in the surface film. When the adult breaks free from
the pupal sheath, it pulls out and flies away. Like caddisflies,
the midge adults aren't very important during the emergence
process because they usually aren't on the water long enough
to create a concentration of insects on the surface.

When the air temperature is cold, it sometimes takes the midge adults longer to get off the water. They skitter and flutter on the surface trying to get their motors running. That's when a high-riding dry fly can interest a feeding trout. Another time that you can expect action from dry flies is when the adult midges come back to mate and lay their eggs. The males are very aggressive and often four or five males clump on one female. A clump of midges hovering and skittering across the surface can really get trout excited. For this I like to use a pattern like a Griffith's Gnat, Improved Buzz Ball, or Renegade.

It doesn't take much skill to tie a midge pupa that works. Tie the fly completely out of thread, making it a little fatter at the thorax area. Or make a more intricate pupa pattern with a quill or goose biot abdomen with dubbing at the thorax. I like to use materials like Antron to brighten the pattern, the same effect you get with a caddis pupa. In fact, many of the same pupal and emerger patterns you use for caddisflies will work equally well tied in smaller sizes—20 to 24—to imitate the midge pupa. The pattern for hyperselective fish is the Halo Midge Emerger. It floats forever, it's easy to see on the water, and with its Antron-dubbed body trout love it. It is a little more complicated to tie but, at least down to size 20, the effort is worthwhile.

One effective way to fish a midge pupa is to attach it as a dropper 8 to 12 inches from a high-floating dry fly like a Griffith's Gnat or a Royal Wulff. You still need to keep the dry fly small because you'll frequently get trout to take it as well as the pupa. Thread the tippet through the top fly and tie on another piece of short tippet with a blood or surgeon's knot. This knot is too fat to pull through the eye of the dry fly. Attach the pupa to the end of the remaining tippet.

Midge fishing gets good on Island Park Reservoir in early June. Work the fingers near the West End Campground. Look for bulging trout during the morning hours. I like the dropper method with a dry fly on top and the pupa underneath. You don't need small midge patterns for this fishing. I normally use a size 12 or 14. It often helps to give the fly a slight twitch when a trout approaches.

Midge fishing is good on the upper Henry's Fork near Last Chance in October and November before the general trout season closes. After that, you'll need to concentrate on the lower river where the fishing is open year-round.

In the old days we spent many a day fishing midges on the river above St. Anthony. It wasn't sophisticated fishing. We tied on a short-shanked size-16 fly with a dark gray body ribbed with fine gold wire and a couple of turns of grizzly hackle clipped short. We called the pattern a Snow Fly. We cast it down and across, allowing it to swing slowly in the current on a tight line. I still use the same technique. I still think it produces more trout during the winter months than any other method.

CHAPTER 7

Terrestrials

Many anglers overlook the importance of terrestrial insects on western trout streams. One reason they are frequently overlooked is that, with the exception of ants, you seldom see a great concentration of hoppers, beetles, crickets, or other terrestrials at any one time. Nonetheless, these types of insects are living near trout streams for the better part of the season and many of them eventually end up in the water. Once they get on the water, they are virtually helpless and make a prime meal for trout.

The Henry's Fork, with its vast meadows, grasslands, and undercut banks, provides ideal habitat for land-based insects. If you plan to fish this river during almost any time of the season without a good supply of terrestrial patterns, you're making a mistake.

BEETLES

If I was only limited to one dry fly that I could use on the Ranch throughout the entire season, I'd have to pick a black beetle in a size 14 or 16. You will find as many beetles

The Black Foam Beetle fooled this nice rainbow. (Photo by Mike Lawson)

on the water out in the middle of river as you will next to the bank, because they are flying insects. There are a number of beetle patterns which are effective. My favorite is a Black Foam Beetle with a peacock herl underbody. You can use elk hair, crystal flash, hackle, or tying thread for legs. Simple to tie, the Black Foam Beetle is durable compared to the deer hair beetles which get torn up after a fish or two. If you want to use hair, try spinning it and then clipping it to shape, leaving a few longer fibers for legs. It looks like a flat, black Irresistible, only without wings, hackle, and tail. The key is to use a fly that will sit in the surface film.

While I usually don't have much success blind casting, the beetle is a great fly to use if there is nothing rising and you want to work down a grassy bank. One of the best times to use a beetle is during a hatch, when the trout are really keyed in on small mayflies or caddisflies. Tossing a beetle pattern over them will almost always get a notice. Try to get a read on the feeding pattern of an individual trout and then make your cast in the trout's feeding rhythm.

ANTS

Throughout any season, the Henry's Fork gets dozens of species of ants falling on the water. They seem to peak in late August and September, but it's tough to predict when they'll be there. One day they'll hit the water and then the next day they won't. You can't depend on when an ant fall is going to happen.

There are several types of ants that are common to the Henry's Fork. The one that gets the trout in a feeding frenzy is a large, plump amber-colored flying ant about a size 12 or 14. It is always accompanied by smaller black flying ants, which are a size 18 or 20. The larger ones are definitely females because their abdomens are loaded with eggs and the small black ones are likely males. I'm not an entomologist so I don't know the species. In fact, I'm not even sure they are actually ants. Some anglers believe they are termites.

What matters is the trout just go bonkers when they hit the water. They act like they haven't eaten for a month when these big ants show up. The trout boil and swirl like there is no tomorrow. But just because they act like gluttons, they aren't easy. You have to have the right pattern.

In the early days of my guiding career, I took my good friend, Jim Barnett, on a fishing trip through the Railroad Ranch. It was still owned by the Harrimans and Jim was a close personal friend of Roland Harriman. I always enjoyed spending time with him because he knew the vision the Harrimans had for this magnificent piece of property. Even today, it helps me better understand the responsibility we have to protect it for generations to come.

We caught some nice trout in the morning on spinners and later on Pale Morning Duns. Around noon the river literally came alive with rising trout. It was exciting to see all the feeding activity and, because we had done well so far, we expected the streak to continue. It wasn't long before our tails were dragging. We couldn't get a notice or even a refusal. I finally put down my rod and got out my little aquarium net. I quickly solved the mystery as to what was causing the feeding frenzy. Those big amber ants were everywhere. The bad news was we didn't have anything even close to match it. We tried clipping some standard dry flies and modifying a No-Hackle, but no luck. The trout just kept feeding and thumbing their noses at us. We finally sat on the bank and laughed at ourselves. Since that day I've never ventured onto the Ranch during July, August, or September without a good supply of big amber ants.

The best pattern I've found to imitate these big flying ants is tied on a standard dry-fly hook with a long, plump abdomen that is half the length of the hook shank. The waist should be slender without dubbing, using only the tan tying thread. Tie in two dark gray CDC feathers mixed with a few strands of Z-Lon extending back past the bend of the hook for the wings. The upper segment should be covered with dubbing on the upper one-fourth of the hook shank. Tie it in size 12 or 14. You can modify this pattern with black in size 18 or 20 for the smaller flying ants. I also like to carry a few Black Fur Ants without wings in size 16, 18, and 20. Foam Ants in the same size and color combination are also good but I like the Fur Ants better because they sit lower in the surface film.

GRASSHOPPERS

Have you ever heard of the grasshopper wind? When the warm afternoon wind blows across lush grasses along a meadow stream and the trout move in to pick up all of the hoppers that get blown in, you'll know the grasshopper wind. The first time I witnessed it was when I was driving across the bridge at Ojo Caliente Geyser on the Firehole River in Yellowstone Park. My brother Rick and I had been driven off the water by a stout south wind. The water exploded just downstream like a bowling ball had been tossed into the water.

We pulled the pickup over and Rick rigged up his rod. He tied on a hopper and looped around below the spot where the trout had erupted. It was a tough cast because there was a stiff wind blowing across his casting arm. He worked his way upstream until he raised the trout. It was a nice brown, bigger than anything I had seen on the Firehole in some time. As he slipped it back into the water, another fish blasted a hopper one hundred feet downstream. The wind had blown another hopper in.

Hoppers are important on the Henry's Fork from mid-July through September. The Harriman Park section receives the most attention because of the vast meadows, but there is good hopper fishing throughout the entire watershed. The tributary streams, most notably Fall River and Teton River, offer excellent possibilities.

There are several important considerations with regard to the tactics of hopper fishing. The best fishing occurs when the wind is blowing. The prevailing wind comes from the south, upstream on the Henry's Fork. The best "hopper banks" are where the wind blows across on the windward side. This makes casting difficult for a right-handed caster if you are working a bank upstream, because it blows the line into your body. You can wade out and work down the bank, but then you'll be casting almost directly into the teeth of the wind. The best way to deal with the wind is to use a heavier rod. Put the three-weight away and rig up a six- or seven-weight rod. Shorten up the leader to 7½ feet. Drive the fly low by making a high back cast and lowering the forward cast.

Using a wind-resistant fly will also help you deal with the wind. I developed the Henry's Fork Hopper to present a better silhouette on the water. It is also aerodynamic and easy to drive into the wind. Once you get it going in the right direction, it continues without being blown off course. You can also cast sidearm and literally skip it under an overhanging bank.

I created this pattern many years ago before there were so many other hopper patterns to choose from. The excellent hopper fishing on the Henry's Fork was a secret shared by only a few regulars. Eventually the trout started getting wise. They began to ignore traditional patterns like the Joe's Hopper and Letort Hopper. These flies looked so good on the water it was difficult to understand why the trout wouldn't take them until I took a couple of naturals home and looked at them from underneath in my aquarium. It was easy to see what was wrong. They sat up on the surface instead of riding down in the surface film. It was a classic case of how trout often see our presentation much differently than we do.

I tied a pattern described in Vince Marinaro's *A Modern Dry Fly Code*, the Pontoon Hopper. It required cutting the tip of the quill from a turkey tail feather, plugging the end, and gluing it on a hook. It was a tedious job but well worth the effort. It worked like a charm. In an effort to reduce the tying time and frustration, I decided to use the same general idea but to make some changes to simplify the tying procedure. The pattern evolved into the Henry's Fork Hopper.

You need some long elk body hair. I like the natural cream-colored, long hair from the rump. Tie it back, wrapping the thread down and past the hook bend. Pull the hair forward and wrap back up the hook, forming a segmented look. The underwing is yellow elk hair with a mottled hen hackle feather or pheasant rump feather as the overwing. I use Dave's Flexament to coat the overwing so it will hold together. Finish the fly with natural gray elk hair as a bullet head. The fly works as well as the Pontoon Hopper but the materials are much more readily available and it is easier to tie. You want sizes from 6 down through 14.

Other hopper imitations, such as Dave's Hopper, work well where better visibility is required. Floating the lower sections of the river during August and September can be productive. Another pattern that produces well and is easy to see is Randall Kaufmann's Stimulator.

Dropping a Black Fur Ant 18 inches below the hopper is a good trick on water that gets more fishing pressure. A trout can't resist an ant even if he decides to refuse the hopper.

CRICKETS

I didn't realize how productive crickets can be until my friend, Barry Beck, gave me a good lesson. I've never noticed them on the water, but Barry hooked plenty of nice trout one day when we fished together on the Ranch. He said he uses them a lot back east and has found them to work equally well out west. Now I always carry a few in my fly box.

I like two patterns. You can tie a modified version of the Henry's Fork Hopper by changing the colors and hook style. Crickets are not as elongated as hoppers so you don't need a long-shank hook. Use brown elk for the body with a black overwing and black elk hair for the bullet head. Another good pattern is a Parachute Cricket, a modification of Ed Schroeder's Parachute Hopper. Crickets are usually smaller than hoppers. My favorite sizes are 14 and 16.

CICADAS

Another fly which works very well on the Henry's Fork, especially in the lower reaches is the Cicada. I don't know why it works so well because I've never seen a natural cicada anywhere near the Henry's Fork. Some of my friends from Utah who fish the Green River first introduced me to it. There are lots of imitations, but I like a simple black foam body with a short wing of light elk hair. Tie your Cicada patterns short and plump. The best sizes are 8 and 10.

CHAPTER 8

Nymphing Methods

he first thing to decide if you're going to fish a nymph is not what the fish are feeding on, but at what depth they're feeding. If you don't find that depth, matching the nymph will be futile. In moving water trout normally hold near or at the bottom, or near or at the surface. When the nymphs are concentrated near the surface during emergence, the trout will be looking for them there. Otherwise, they'll be holding near the bottom where they don't expend much energy swimming against the current.

The most difficult place to fish nymphs on the Henry's Fork is in the really flat water of places like Railroad Ranch. The simplest way to deal with the flat water is to use a strike indicator. You don't need much weight to get the nymph down in the slow-moving flat water. The indicator should be small. There are several good commercial indicators including the soft foam stick-on indicators. Another good indicator is a one-inch section of bright fly line with the core pulled out. This indicator was first developed by Dave Whitlock. The advantage of the fly-line indicator is you can slide it up or down the leader to keep it at the proper distance from the fly. Most of the water in the Ranch is about 3 feet in depth so I usually keep the indicator 4 or 5 feet above the fly.

You can also use a dry fly as an indicator. This is particularly effective when the fish are feeding on nymphs near or at the surface. I like to keep the nymph within a foot or so of the dry fly when I'm trying to keep the nymph near the surface.

Distinguishing between surface rises and close-to-the-surface rises can sometimes be a problem. I look for a bubble. Usually when the fish pokes his nose out and takes a fly on the surface, he gets a little bit of air in his mouth and when he goes back down, he'll expel that air and there'll be a little bubble. If you watch a fish consistently breaking the surface film but you never see a bubble, then you can assume that he is probably taking nymphs just under the surface film.

Emergers are among the most effective patterns on the river, particularly on the Ranch. Fish them right in the surface film. Most of the surface activity on a spring creek is going to be in three different areas: on the surface, in the surface, or just under the surface. But keep in mind that the surface layer of water is one inch deep.

Another good way to catch trout on nymphs in the clear water of the Henry's Fork is to sight fish. Sight fishing means you stalk the water until you spot a fish. You need to learn to look into the water, not at it. Trout are not easy to see because they are well camouflaged against the bottom. Look for the movement of a tail, shadows, or the opening of a trout's white mouth. Work slowly and cautiously. You can look at the same section of water for several minutes until you spot the telltale sign of a trout.

Once you spot a fish, stalk into casting position. You can get much closer if you work up from below. This method won't work unless you can actually see the trout react to your

fly. Don't watch your line, leader, or an indicator. Only watch
the fish. This means you'll normally need to work to within
about 15 feet of the trout. Once you get into casting position,
watch the trout a few minutes. Usually they will be aware of
your presence but will settle down when they realize you pose
them no danger. During the observation period you might
see the trout move to one side or the other, taking a nymph.
You won't be able to see the take if you drift the fly right into
the trout's holding position. If you cast a foot to eighteen
inches to the side of the trout's feeding lane, you'll know he's
going for your fly when you see him move over. Wait for him
to start to move back before you tighten. Trout take nymphs
very softly in slow water. Don't set hard or you'll spook the
fish if he didn't take your fly. Just tighten firmly and deliber-
ately and when the trout feels the resistance, he'll be hooked.

If you're in doubt about the exact size and color of the
predominant nymphs, a Pheasant Tail Nymph is a good
searching pattern. Its color scheme will imitate a lot of different mayflies, but you better have a wide assortment of sizes
because that's where the trout will get most selective.

Fishing nymphs in the faster water sections of the river
requires a change in tactics. The "high stick" method,
detailed in the Box Canyon section, works well if you're fishing rough water because you can keep the line tight enough
to feel your nymph tick across the bottom while lifting and
lowering the rod tip as needed to feed the weighted nymph
into the deeper pockets between the rocks. This tactic is
deadly when you're wading areas like the Box Canyon.

I do not like sinking lines for fishing nymphs in rivers
and streams. I lose a degree of line control with sinking lines.
For that reason, I use a floating line for all of my nymph fishing on the Henry's Fork. For short-line nymphing, I frequently
use a fly line one size heavier than recommended for the rod.
My favorite setup is a nine-foot, five-weight rod with a size-6

floating line. The heavier line helps load the rod better when making short casts.

It's hard to beat an indicator if you are floating and fishing from a drift boat. The size and kind of indicator needed depends a lot on the type of water you're fishing as well as how much weight you're using. I don't like heavily weighted nymphs. I would rather have the option of adding more weight to the tippet to help get the fly down deep.

In heavy water there are a couple of options you can use to help get the fly deep. If I need more weight, my first preference is to add a second weighted nymph. I tie a section of tippet directly to the first nymph, either at the eye or bend of the hook, with a clinch knot. Then I add a second nymph as a dropper. I like to keep the two nymphs between 12 and 18 inches apart.

If I still need more weight to keep the flies down, I can add a split shot about 12 inches above the top fly. I've tried adding the extra weight between the two nymphs but the dropper section can tangle badly if I hook a trout on the top fly.

I like to use extra weight which can be easily added or taken away. I prefer the removable split shot. I have trouble getting flat lead strips like twist-ons to stay in place.

In recent years there has been a movement to stop using lead for fishing, because it is toxic to waterfowl and other animals. Lead weight is currently illegal to use in Yellowstone National Park. I personally don't have a problem with it because ducks and geese don't feed in the sections of fast water where you need additional weight. There are alternatives to lead, however. Several companies manufacture non-toxic split shots and they are available in all of the fly fishing shops in and around West Yellowstone.

I have recently discovered that the natural color of lead can actually put off a trout. Trout see a lot of lead split shot in water like the Box Canyon. It's the same rationale as when trout keep seeing the same pattern too much. Eventually they wise up and won't take it. A lead split shot really stands out. The Dinsmore company manufactures nontoxic weight which is dark green in color. You can buy it in a five-pack assortment. The dark green color completely camouflages the split shot as it drifts through the water. My first experience with this stuff was fishing the clear streams of New Zealand that have the most spooky and skittish trout in the world. I'm convinced it made a lot of difference in my success rate.

You can also increase the weight needed to get the fly down by using beadhead nymphs. They came here from Europe and it wasn't long before beadhead nymphs became the rage of the nymph-fishing world. You can tie any traditional nymph in a beadhead version. Just slide the bead up to the hook before you start tying the fly.

The beadhead offers a couple of advantages. It provides additional weight to keep the fly down and its brightness may provide some additional attractiveness to the nymph. Even more importantly, the compact weight at the eye of the hook gives the fly an up-and-down, jigging action as it drifts through the water.

Beads come in a variety of colors. I prefer the gold beads but I also use black. Tungsten beads are much heavier and more expensive than standard beads but they can provide a distinct advantage when you need additional weight to get the fly down. I always carry extra tungsten beads in my vest. I thread the leader through a tungsten bead between the top fly and the dropper, allowing the bead to slide free. It is a great alternative to using a split shot and it really works.

I don't worry too much about using nymphs that are exact imitations. My "basic six" for almost all of my nymph fishing on the Henry's Fork includes: Black Rubber Legs (size 4–12), Prince Nymphs (size 10–18), Pheasant Tail Nymphs (size 12–20), Gold-Ribbed Hare's Ears (size 12–18), Green Caddis Larvae (size 12–18), and Green Drake Nymphs (size 10–16). I tie them in traditional and beadhead versions.

CHAPTER 9

Dry Fly Methods

ou need two kinds of dry flies for fishing the Henry's Fork. I've discussed the hatches in detail and many of the patterns needed to imitate them. You also need an assortment of attractor patterns. Match-the-hatch patterns are essential if you expect to catch the selective trout of the Harriman Park and other flat-water stretches of the river. In fast-water stretches, your most important consideration is being able to see the fly and making sure that it's floating.

On fast water, fly selection can be fairly simple. If you use a Royal Wulff or Humpy or Elk Hair Caddis when the fish are rising, most of the time you're going to catch fish. That approach works especially well down in the lower sections of the Henry's Fork near Ashton. Even in the really flat sections of the river below Ashton, you can use these kinds of patterns more often. And you can use a traditional upstream approach and just cast the fly right straight upstream over the fish.

In the flat-water stretches like Harriman Park, it is important to get the fly to drift over the fish before the leader. I like

118

to use a reach cast so you can throw some slack upstream ahead of the fly. After you have completed the power phase of your forward cast and while the line is going forward, point your rod tip upstream. It's just like mending the line in the air.

Another good method that I use a lot is to feed line down to the fish. I just shake the tip of the rod tip briskly while it's close to the water and let the slack run out of my hands. With some practice, you can learn to feed your entire fly line out of the rod without causing any drag on the fly. Avoid standing directly above the fish with this shaking technique, because you'll spook him when you pick the line up to make the next cast.

Setting the hook can be difficult when fishing downstream because you're pulling the fly straight back upstream out of the fish's mouth when he rises. Make sure you give him time to take the fly in his mouth and turn down with it before you strike. Make a slower, more deliberate hook set instead of yanking back with the more common "ninja" hook set.

There are some excellent anglers on the Ranch who like to approach the fish from directly behind. This approach allows you to get very close to the fish and to avoid drag. One problem with this approach, aside from the obvious one of lining the fish and spooking him, is that the fish can miss the fly simply because the leader is in the way. When he lifts his nose against the leader, it pushes the fly away. You can avoid this by getting slightly to the side and below a rising trout.

One of my pet peeves is anglers who use tippets that are too light. I think a lot of fish get killed because anglers play them too long. Nowadays, with modern leader materials, you can use a much lighter tippet than you could twenty years ago because they have such a high breaking strength. In fact, a 6X tippet is now almost twice as strong as it used to be. The problem is, some anglers don't realize how much pressure they can put on a big fish to land him within a reasonable amount of time. They let the fish play them instead of the other way around. The longer you play a trout, the more likely it is to die after it is released.

A good rule to determine the right tippet size to use is to divide the size of your fly by a factor of 3. This means you should use 5X with a size-16 fly and 7X with a size-22. I must admit, however, that I almost never use 7X, even with the smallest of flies.

When you get a strike, light tippet or not, keep the rod tip high. No matter what part of the river you're fishing, whether it's in the Ranch or downstream in the Ashton area, fish are going to break off in the weeds unless you can keep your rod tip high. Once you get past the first initial runs and jumps, you can land the fish if you keep the pressure on. Don't make the mistake of chasing a big fish down the river if you can avoid it. There's no better way to get on the list of "America's Most Wanted" in the Harriman State Park than to chase a fish through another angler's fishing area. If you can't move the trout to you, break him off.

I've talked extensively about patterns to match the various food forms on the Henry's Fork. I also like to carry a box of attractor patterns which are very useful. Here are some of my favorites: Royal Wulffs (size 10–20), Parachute Adams (size 10–22), Olive Humpies (size 10–20), Kaufmann's Tan Stimulators (size 8–14), Renegades (size 12–20), and Royal Trudes (size 10–16). My "basic six" for almost all of my nymph fishing on the Henry's Fork includes: Black Rubber Legs (size 4–12), Prince Nymphs (size 10–18), Pheasant Tail Nymphs (size 12–20), Gold-Ribbed Hare's Ears (size 12–18), Green Caddis Larvae (size 12–18), and Green Drake Nymphs (size 10–16). I tie them in traditional and bead-head versions.

CHAPTER 10

Streamer Methods

I like to separate streamers into two categories—flies that imitate sculpins, minnows, and other forage fish, and flies that represent leeches, crayfish, and other swimming food forms.

There are thousands of leeches on the Henry's Fork. While there is some variation in color and size, I think the action is a lot more important than the pattern. Most of the time, you will find natural leeches in three color schemes—black, dark brown, or dark olive. So stick to these color schemes with your patterns. To get the right action, put a little split shot right at the eye of the hook; they swim with an undulating movement, and you want to get a jigging action on your fly. You can also use a beadhead or a conehead version. I also carry some coneheads in my vest which I can thread with the tippet when I tie on the fly.

The primary objective when fishing streamers is to try to give the fish a broadside look at the fly. Remember, fish always face into the current. If you can make the streamer track across the current, it will give the fish a broadside view.

Wide open vistas on the Henry's Fork are a bonus to the exceptional fishery. (Photo by Barry and Cathy Beck)

If you strip the fly back upstream, into the current, the fish is only going to view the fly from directly below.

You need to learn to control the line during the retrieve in order to accomplish a broadside drift. Cast across and slightly upstream, and as the line drifts downstream, mend by throwing line downstream with the current. It's kind of like trying to scratch your head while you're rubbing your stomach. You need to mend line as you are making the retrieve.

You can also use the rod both to help impart action to the fly or to speed or slow the retrieve. Twitch the rod tip and impart a jigging, up-and-down motion to the fly. You can also slowly lift the rod to help speed up the retrieve or lower it to slow the fly down. Try to tease and entice the trout into a strike.

I do not like to use a full sinking line for streamer fishing on moving water. In most of the sections of the river, including the Box Canyon, a beadhead fly or split shot can usually provide enough weight to keep the fly down with a floating line. I frequently use a sink-tip line, especially during the autumn and early spring. With a sink-tip, I don't need to weight the fly as heavily, so it's easier to cast.

You can buy sink-tips in a wide variety of sinking lengths and sink rates. In shallow water, like the Box Canyon, I use a line with a 6-foot sinking section which is extra fast sinking. My preference for the deep pools of the lower river is a 250-grain, 30-foot head which goes down like a rock. It's a bitch to cast, but you can really get a big streamer down where the big boys hang out.

The most important consideration when using a sink-tip line is to use a short leader. If you use a long leader with a sink-tip line, the fly will track much higher in the current than the line tip. I tie a butt section of about .021 inches in diameter directly to the tip of the line with a perfection loop

18 inches or so below the line tip. Then I loop a 2-foot section of tippet material directly to the loop of the butt section. This makes the total leader length only 3½ feet.

There is no doubt in my mind that if you are trying to catch the biggest trout in the river, streamer fishing is the way to go. When my children were young, Sheralee and I took them on a float through the Harriman State Park the day before it closed. We wanted to get one last look at my favorite place on earth before the season closed on September 30.

We floated over a large school of whitefish and I pointed them out to my youngest son, Chris. Suddenly, I saw a monster rainbow moving among the whitefish. I didn't mess with him because I knew he was spooked.

The following day our oldest son, Shaun, went down in the Ranch with Rob Van Kirk to fish the final day of the season. They sat along the bank and watched for that big trout when the Mahogany Duns started emerging. Even though there were some big trout feeding, they couldn't see the monster we found the day before. Finally, Rob tied on a streamer.

There was a deep pocket just out from the bank where the school of whitefish were holding. Rob tied on a silver Zonker and cast above, letting the current carry the streamer into the deeper water. When Rob started the retrieve, the rod was almost jolted out of his hand. The big rainbow erupted and shot across the river, pushing a giant wake as he went. After a long battle, he finally landed a rainbow that was well over ten pounds.

Shaun took a photo of Rob's trout just before it was released. He gave me a copy which I still treasure. It is one of my most memorable fish, even if I didn't catch it myself.

Some people find streamer fishing dull and boring. They simply cast the fly across and retrieve it back. For me, streamer fishing is relaxing and enjoyable. It is the only form of fly fishing where you don't need to watch the water. You can cast out, work your fly back, and enjoy what this wonderful river has to offer. You might see a bald eagle keeping a close eye on the river below, or a busy water ouzel dipping under the water in search of nymphs. There are river otters, mink, muskrat, and beavers along with a wide variety of waterfowl. You might glance behind you and see a giant bull moose or a whitetail doe and her fawn. In the distance loom the Grand Tetons, the most awe-inspiring mountains on the continent. And best of all, just when you've been overtaken by the majesty of it all, you just might hook a trout of a lifetime.

Appendix 1

Hatch Chart

Mayflies

Blue-Winged Olive	*Baetis tricaudatus & Diphetor hageni*
Hook = 18, Body = olive, Wing = dark gray	
Western March Brown	*Rithrogena morrisoni*
Hook = 12, Body = purplish black, Wing = grayish brown	
Pale Morning Dun	*Ephemerella inermis*
Hook = 18–20, Body = yellowish olive, Wing = light gray	
Western Green Drake	*Drunella grandis*
Hook = 10–12, Body = dark olive, Wing = dark gray	
Brown Drake	*Ephemerella simulans*
Hook = 12–14, Body = yellowish brown, Wing = gray	
Gray Drake	*Siphlonurus occidentalis*
Hook = 10, Body = grayish brown, Wing = gray	
Small Western Green Drake	*Drunella flavilinea*
Hook = 14–16, Body = dark olive, Wing = dark gray	
Speckled Spinner	*Callibaetis nigritus*
Hook = 14–16, Body = olive brown, Wing = gray	
Trico	*Tricorythodes minutus*
Hook = 20–22, Body = blackish brown, Wing = white	
Tiny Blue-Winged Olive	*Baetis punctiventris*
Hook = 22–24, Body = olive, Wing = gray	
Mahogany Dun	*Paraleptophlebia bicornuta*
Hook = 16, Body = mahogany brown, Wing = gray	

Caddisflies

Grannom	*Brachycentrus americanus & B. occidentalis*
Hook = 12–14, Body = greenish brown, Wing = brown to gray	
Spotted Sedge	*Hydropsyche occidentalis & H. cockerelli*
Hook = 10–14, Body = yellowish brown, Wing = tan to brown	
Little Western Weedy Water Sedge	*Amiocentrus aspilus*
Hook = 18–20, Body = greenish brown, Wing = dark brown	

The weeks marked on this chart indicate the heavy hatch periods for each insect. The brief color and size descriptions of the adult stages will allow you to carry at least generally matching patterns.

JAN	FEB	MAR	APRIL	MAY	JUNE	JULY	AUG	SEPT	OCT	NOV	DEC
		•••	••••	••••	••	•••	••	••••	••••	•••	
			••••	••••							
				•	••••	••••	••••	••••	••		
					•••	•					
					••	••					
					•••	••					
					••	••••	•				
						••••	••••	••			
						•	••••	••••			
							•••	••••	••		
							•	••••	•••		
			••••	•••		•	••••	••			
				•	••••	•••	•	••••			
					••••	••••					

CADDISFLIES (CONT.)

LONG-HORN SEDGE	*Oecetis disjuncta & O. avara*
Hook = 12–14, Body = ginger to brown, Wing = tan to brown	

LITTLE SISTER SEDGE	*Cheumatopsyche campyla*
Hook = 14–16, Body = ginger to brown, Wing = tan to brown	

SPECKLED PETER	*Helicopsyche borealis*
Hook = 18, Body = straw yellow, Wing = speckled brown	

BLACK DANCER	*Mystacides alafimbriata*
Hook = 14–16, Body = yellowish, Wing = black	

AUTUMN MOTTLED SEDGE	*Neophylax rickeri*
Hook = 8–10, Body = brownish yellow, Wing = mottled brown	

STONEFLIES

SALMON FLY	*Pteronarcys californica*
Hook = 2–6, Body = orange, Wing = dark gray	

GOLDEN STONE	*Calineuria californica*
Hook = 6–8, Body = light ginger, Wing = ginger	

LITTLE OLIVE	*Alloperla* species
Hook = 14–16, Body = bright green, Wing = light gray	

YELLOW SALLY	*Isoperla* species
Hook = 14–16, Body = bright green, Wing = light gray	

DAMSELFLIES

DAMSEL	*Enallagma* species
Hook = 6–10, Nymph = olive to brown	
COMMENTS: Emergence period on Henry's Lake.	

TWO-WINGED FLIES

MIDGES	Diptera species
Hook = 16–28, Body = red, olive, gray, Wing = clear	

JAN	FEB	MAR	APRIL	MAY	JUNE	JULY	AUG	SEPT	OCT	NOV	DEC
				•	••••	••••	•				
					•••	••••					
					•••						
						•••	••••				
							••••	•			
				•••	•••						
				•	••••	••••					
					••••	•					
				•	••••	••					
				•	•••						
••••	••••	••••	••						••••	••••	••••

APPENDIX 2

Popular Flies for the Henry's Fork

|T| reat this list as a framework rather than a must-have set of flies. Work from it to fill your boxes during the winter, or if you don't tie, purchase a workable selection. You will not need all of these patterns at any given time or on any given section of the river. You can match how, when, and where you intend to fish to put together your own pattern list. Shops in the area sell all of these flies and many are available through mail order.

Should you bring favorite patterns from your home waters? Absolutely. A good fly will work anywhere. The same imitations and attractors that fool trout in the East, West, or South will take the rainbows and browns of the Henry's Fork. At the same time, don't ignore the local killers—flies that have proven themselves on the river.

DRY FLIES AND EMERGERS

MAYFLY IMITATIONS

No-Hackle Duns (for flat water)
Slate/Olive 14–18   Gray/Yellow 16–20   Gray/Olive 18–22
Slate/Tan 14–20   White/Black 0–22

Thorax Duns (for rough water)
PMD 16–20   BWO 18–22   Trico 20–22
Western Olive 14–20   Mahogany 14–18

Sparkle Duns
PMD 16–18   Slate/Olive 14–16   Mahogany Dun 16–18
Baetis 20–22

Paradrake and Green Drake Wulff 8–12 (tie to match olive body and gray wing
                                           of Green Drake)

Mike's Brown Drake 10
Mike's Gray Drake 10–12
Mike's Green Drake 10–12
Hen Wing Spinners
PMD 16–20   Rusty 14–20   Trico 20–22
Green Drake 10–12   Brown Drake 10   Gray Drake 10–12
Callibaetis **Partridge Spinner** 14–16
Brown Drake Spinner 10–12
Green Drake Cripple 10–12
Brown Drake Cripple 10–12
Mayfly Cripple PMD 16–20
Limestone Cripple 16–18

DRY FLIES AND EMERGERS – MAYFLY (CONT.)

Brown Drake Emerger   10
Dr. Bar Emerger   PMD 16–18
Half Back Emerger   PMD 16–18   BWO 20–22
Shroud   12–16
Standards
Quill Gordon 12–16   Red Quill 16–20   Adams 10–16

CADDISFLY IMITATIONS

Hemingway Special and Henryville   12–18
Elk Hair Caddis   10–16 (dark and light versions, also use in appropriate colors to
                                  cover hatches matched by Yellow Sally or Little Olive Stone)
Dancing Caddis   Ginger 12
Peacock Caddis   12–16
Spent Partridge Caddis   12–20 (olive, tan, peacock)
E-Z Caddis   Olive 14–18   Tan 14-18
Partridge Caddis Emerger   14–18 (tan, olive)
Emergent Sparkle Pupa   8–18 (bright green, amber, dark gray)

STONEFLY IMITATIONS

Fluttering Stone   4–8 (high riding)
Henry's Fork Salmon Fly   4–8 (low riding)
Henry's Fork Golden   6–12
Henry's Fork Yellow Sally   12–16
Improved Sofa Pillow   4–8
Kaufmann's Stimulator   Orange 4–6   Tan 8–12
Bird's Stone   4–8 (fish dry or trim and fish wet as modern substitute for the old
                          Triple Bar X)

OTHER INSECT IMITATIONS

Griffith's Gnat   18–24
Gray Hackle Midge   16–24
Halo Midge Emerger   Black 16–20   Olive/Red 18–20
Improved Buzz Ball   14–16
Snow Fly   18–20

TERRESTRIAL IMITATIONS

Black Foam Beetle   10–12
Henry's Fork Hopper 6–14
Henry's Fork Cricket 12–16
Parachute Hopper   Tan 8–12
Parachute Cricket   10–16
Dave's Hopper   6–12
Crowe Beetle   10–20 (use elk hair for durability)
Brown Flying Ant   12–16 (matches large termite)
Black Flying Ant   14–20
Cinnamon Flying Ant   14–20
Black Fur Ant   14–20
Foam Ant   Black 12–16   Red 16–18
Foam Cicada   6–14

DRY FLIES and EMERGERS – Terrestrial (cont.)

Chernobyl Ant   8–12

Turck's Tarantula   4–8

> Pine bark beetles infesting nearby forests provide a major food source, so small beetle imitations work consistently.

Rough Water Patterns

Stimulator   8–14 (royal, black)

Parachute Adams   10–20

Royal Wulff   10–18

Madam X   10–20

Goofus   10–16

Irresistible   10–16

H & L Variant   10–16

Humpy   Yellow 10–18   Olive 10–20

Royal Trude   6–16

Renegade   10–20

High Riding Exciters

Dun Variant   12–16

Skating Spider   10–16 (cream and grizzly colors)

NYMPHS

Mayfly Imitations

Brown Drake Nymph   8–10

Green Drake Nymph   10–12

PMD Nymph   14–18

Callibaetis Swimming Nymph   14–16

Floating Nymphs   PMD 16–18   Tan 16–20   Olive 14–22

Caddisfly Imitations

Beadhead Electric Caddis   12–16 (green, cream)

Peeking Caddis   10–14 (cream and olive)

Deep Sparkle Pupa   8–18 (bright green, amber, dark gray)

Cased Caddis Larva   6–14 (dark colors)

Caddis Larva   12–16 (green, cream)

Free-Living Caddis Larva   Bright Green 12–16

Stonefly Imitations

Pale Cream Stone Fly Nymph   2–8 (tie like Montana Nymph but with cream chenille)

Kaufmann Black Stone   2–8

Brooks Stone   2–8

Black Rubber Legs Nymph   4–6

Lawson Golden Stone   8–10

Other Imitations

Whitlock Damsel   6–10 (olive and brown)

Floating Damsel   6–8

NYMPHS – Other (cont.)

Kaufmann Scud   8–14
Variegated Midge Larva   18–24

General

Prince Nymph   8–16 (with and without beadhead)
Copper John Nymph   12–18
Woolly Worm   4–10 (brown, olive, fluorescent green)
Pheasant Tail Nymph   12–18   Beadhead 16–18
Hare's Ear   10–16
Gold-Ribbed Hare's Ear   10–16 (with and without beadhead)
Serendipity   12–18 (olive, tan, red)
Girdle Bug   2–8
Yuk Bug   2–8

STREAMERS

Imitators

Double Bunny   Gray/White 2–4
Kiwi Muddler   2–8
Conehead Rabbit Leech   Black/Olive 2–6
Wool Head Sculpin   2–6 (black and olive)
Mohair Leech   2–6 (olive, black, brown, red, purple)
Bunny Leech   2–6 (black, brown, dark olive)

Attractors

Halloween Woolly Bugger (for lakes)
Glo Bug   8–12 (pink and orange for autumn rainbow runs above Island Park)
Flasha-Bugger   2–6
Zonker   2–10 (olive pearlescent variations for matching young Kokanee Salmon spit
            through Island Park Dam)

General

Woolly Bugger   4–8 (black, olive)
Conehead Bugger   4–8 (black, olive)
Matuka   2–10 (olive, natural grizzly)
Muddler Minnow   2–10
Clouser Minnow   4–6 (tan/white, gray/white)
Marabou Muddler   2–10 (white, black, brown)
        Island Park Reservoir is rich with small crayfish that many fly
        anglers overlook. Imitating them might be worth a try.

Wet Flies

Brown Drake Soft Hackle   10–12
Krystal Bugger   6–10 (black, peacock, olive)
Diving Blue-Winged Olive Egg Layer   16–18
Diving Caddis   12–18 (brown/yellow, brown/green, green, ginger)

Appendix 3

Recipes for Twelve Key Flies

Flies photographed by Randall Kaufmann
(except fly number 2, photographed by Doug O'looney)

1. Black Foam Beetle

Hook	TMC 100, sizes 14–18
Thread	Black, 3/0
Back	Black foam
Underbody	Peacock herl (optional)
Legs	Black deer

2. Diving Blue-Winged Olive Egg Layer

Hook	Mustad 3906, sizes 14–22
Thread	Olive, 8/0
Weight	A strip of fine lead or bismuth wire under the thorax
Tails	Medium dun hackle fibers
Abdomen	Olive synthetic dubbing
Thorax	Olive synthetic dubbing (thicker)
Wing	Clear Antron fibers tied back at a 45-degree angle
Hackle	Medium dun hackle fibers (beard style)

3. Emergent Sparkle Pupa – Bright Green

Hook	TMC 100, sizes 12–18
Thread	Black, 6/0
Overbody	Bright green Antron yarn
Underbody	Bright green Antron yarn
Wing	Natural deer
Head	Dark brown Superfine

4. HALF BACK EMERGER
Blue-Winged Olive

HOOK	TMC 100, sizes 18, 20
THREAD	Olive, 6/0
SHUCK	Brown Z-Lon
RIB	Red copper wire, fine
ABDOMEN	Pheasant tail
WINGCASE	Medium gray deer
THORAX	Olive Superfine

5. HENRY'S FORK GOLDEN STONE

HOOK	TMC 5262, sizes 8, 10
THREAD	Tan, 3/0
TAIL	Dark tan elk
HACKLE	Brown, palmered and trimmed
BODY	Yellow-tan elk
WING	Light tan elk
HEAD	Dark tan elk tied bullet head style

6. HENRY'S FORK HOPPER

HOOK	TMC 5212, sizes 6–14
THREAD	Yellow, 3/0
BODY	Natural cream elk rump, reverse style, extended
UNDERWING	Yellow elk
OVERWING	Mottled brown hen saddle feather coated with Dave's Flexament
HEAD	Natural gray elk, tied bullet head style
LEGS	Light yellow rubber

7. HENRY'S FORK SALMON FLY

HOOK   TMC 5262, sizes 4, 6

THREAD   Fluorescent fire
orange, 6/0

TAIL   Black moose

HACKLE   Brown, palmered
and trimmed

BODY   Brownish orange elk

WING   Dark gray elk

HEAD   Black elk tied bullet-
head style

8. NO-HACKLE
Slate Tan

HOOK   TMC 100 or 5210,
sizes 14–18

THREAD   Dark brown, 6/0

TAIL   Dark dun hackle
fibers

BODY   Tan Superfine

WING   Dark gray mallard
quill

9. PHEASANT TAIL NYMPH

HOOK   TMC 3761, sizes
10–20, weighted

THREAD   Brown, 6/0

TAIL   Ringneck pheasant
tail

RIB   Copper wire, fine

ABDOMEN   Ringneck pheasant
tail

BODY   Tan Superfine

WINGCASE   Ringneck pheasant
tail fibers; tips form legs

THORAX   Peacock

10. PRINCE NYMPH

HOOK TMC 5263, sizes 6–18
WEIGHT Lead wire, diameter of hook shank
THREAD Black, 6/0
TAIL Brown goose or turkey biot
ABDOMEN Peacock
LEGS Brown or furnace hackle
WING White goose biot

11. RUSTY HEN SPINNER

HOOK TMC 100 or 5210, sizes 14–18
THREAD Brown, 6/0
WING Light dun hen hackle tips, tied spent
TAIL Medium dun hackle fibers, split
BODY Rusty brown Superfine

12. SPENT PARTRIDGE CADDIS, Peacock

HOOK TMC 00, sizes 14–18
THREAD Olive, 6/0
BODY Peacock herl
WING Dark brown mottled partridge feathers
HACKLE Brown and grizzly

APPENDIX 4

The Henry's Fork Foundation

*I*n 1984, founder William R. Manlove organized the Henry's Fork Foundation (HFF). Proposals for four hydro-projects that threatened to dewater large portions of the Henry's Fork provided the impetus for organizing the new group. Mike Lawson was one of the original members.

The foundation secured federal legislation to protect sections of the river from further hydroelectric development and lobbied for and received strict environmental guidelines for licensing a hydro-project at the existing Island Park Dam. The added facility actually improves the water quality below the dam.

In ensuing years, HFF has worked to reduce livestock grazing impacts to the Harriman State Park section of the river (also known as Railroad Ranch) by funding and installing twenty-one miles of solar-powered electric fence to control the cattle. Other cooperative efforts have led to the installation of a fish ladder on the Buffalo River, tighter "catch and release" regulations on the Harriman Park and Box Canyon sections, and strict slot limits on most of the remainder of the river. The foundation is active in protecting open space along the entire river corridor and has funded extensive research to better understand the complexities of the Henry's Fork watershed.

In the past several years, HFF has conducted a habitat assessment of the river and stream corridors in the entire watershed funded with a challenge grant from the National Fish and Wildlife Foundation, has steadily increased efforts in the areas of rehabilitation and restoration of stream connectivity and viable fish habitat, and has worked with appropriate management agencies in their efforts to preserve and protect native fish in the Henry's Fork drainage. Through a major grant from the Ford Foundation, HFF is working on several fronts in the arena of community-based conservation, educating and supporting all watershed users in their efforts to enjoy a high quality of life.

HFF recently worked with state and federal agencies, as well as irrigators and other resource users, to form the Henry's Fork Watershed Council. This multi-interest forum meets to better understand a variety of natural resource management concerns and to find common ground to better protect the river for all citizens.

For more information, write to Janice Brown, Executive Director, Henry's Fork Foundation, 606 Main St., Ashton, ID 83420, call (208) 652-3567, or e-mail: hff@henrysfork.com. Also visit their web site: www.henrysfork.com.

SUGGESTED READING

BOOKS

Arnold, Paul. *Wisdom of the Guides: Rocky Mountain Trout Guides Talk Fly Fishing*. Portland: Frank Amato Publications, 1998.

Brooks, Charles E. *The Henry's Fork*. New York: NIck Lyons, 1986.

Kaufmann, Randall. *Patterns of the Umpqua Feather Merchants*. Glide, Oregon: Umpqua Feather Merchants, 1998.

Knopp, Malcolm, and Robert Cormier. *Mayflies: An Angler's Study of Trout Water Ephemeroptera*. Helena, Montana: Greycliff Publishing Company, 1997.

LaFontaine, Gary. *Caddisflies*. New York: Lyons and Burford, 1981.

LaFontaine, Gary. *Trout Flies: Proven Patterns*. Helena, Montana: Greycliff Publishing Company, 1993.

Marinaro, Vincent. *A Modern Dry Fly Code*. 1950; reprint, New York: Lyons Press, 1997.

Retallic, Ken, and Rocky Barker. *Flyfisher's Guide to Idaho*. Gallatin Gateway, Montana: Wilderness Adventures Press, 1996.

Schiess, Bill. *Fishing Henry's Lake*. Mountain Home, Idaho: Bill Schiess, 1988.

Shewey, John. *Mastering the Spring Creeks: A Fly Angler's Guide*. Portland, Oregon: Frank Amato Publications, 1994.

Staples, Bruce. *Snake River Country: Flies and Waters*. Portland, Oregon: Frank Amato Publications, 1991.

Swisher, Doug, and Carl Richards. *Selective Trout*. 1971; reprint, New York: Lyons Press, 1989.

Thomas, Greg. *Best Flies for Idaho*. Helena, Montana: Greycliff Publishing Company, 2000.

Tullis, Larry. *Henry's Fork*. River Journal Series. Portland, Oregon: Frank Amato Publications, 1995.

AUDIO TAPE

Lawson, Mike, and Gary LaFontaine. *Fly Fishing the Henry's Fork*. River Rap Series. Helena, Montana: Greycliff Publishing Company, 1987.

INDEX

Adams, 131
air bubbles 75, 113
Alloperla species, 128
American Grannom, 76
Amiocentrus aspilus, 77, 126
Antron, 74, 76-77, 83, 98, 102-103, 107-108
ants, 26, 39, 107, 111, 131-132
Arbona, Fred, Jr., ix
Arctopsyche grandis, 70
Ashton, 38, 52-53, 60, 67, 76, 84, 91, 99, 118, 120
Ashton Dam, 40-42, 52, 94-95
Ashton Reservoir, 38-40
Autumn Mottled Sedge, 128
autumn, 61- 62

Bacon, Gil and Arlene, 36
Baetis, 1, 55, 59, 81-83, 126, 130
Baetis parvus. See Diphetor hageni
Baetis punctiventris, 82, 126
Baetis tricaudatis, 82-83, 126
Bailey, Dan, 91
bait fish, 60
Barnes, Pat, 90-91
Barnett, Jim, 107
Beadhead Electric Caddis, 132
Beadhead Pheasant Tail, 23, 133
beads, 116
Bear Gulch, 33
Bechler Ranger Station, 47
Bechler River, 47
Beck, Barry, 111
beetles, 60, 105-106
Big Sky, Montana, 53
Big Springs, 12-13

Bill Schiess, 9
Bird's Stonefly, 21, 68, 69, 131
Black Beetle, 26, 105
Black Dancer, 80, 128
Black Flying Ant, 131
Black Foam Beetle, 106, 131, 134
Black Fur Ant, 108, 111, 131
Black Quill. *See* Western March Brown.
Black Rubber Legs Nymph, 19, 66, 116, 120
blind fishing, 3, 51, 106
Blue-Winged Olive, 41, 48, 55, 59, 61, 81-83, 99, 126
boats, 7-8, 13, 17, 22, 24, 33, 35-36, 39, 42, 71, 90, 115
Bonefish Flats, 24, 79, 80, 99
Boundary Creek, 47
Box Canyon, 6, 16, 17-24, 39, 40, 45, 65, 69, 114, 116, 123, 138
Brachycentrus americanus, 55, 126
Brachycentrus occidentalis, 56
Bradshaw, Stan, ix
Brassie, 102
brook trout, 6, 7, 10, 37, 46-47, 62
Brooks, Charles, 25
Brooks Stone, 66, 132
Brown Drake, 13, 27, 50, 59, 91-93, 95, 126
Brown Drake Cripple, 130
Brown Drake Emerger, 131
Brown Drake Nymph, 92, 132
Brown Drake Soft Hackle Emerger, 92, 133
Brown Drake Spinner, 92, 130
Brown Flying Ant, 131

141

brown trout, 36, 38, 45, 47, 53, 54, 62, 71, 130
Brown, Cecil, 12
Brown, Janice, 139
Brown, Paul, ix
Buffalo Campground, 46
Buffalo River, 19, 45-46, 64-65, 91, 138
Bunny Leech, 133
Bureau of Land Management, 43

Caddis Emerger, 76, 77
Caddis Larva, 132
Caddisflies, by Gary LaFontaine, ix, 72-73
caddisflies, 18, 27, 28, 38, 41, 42, 50, 55-57, 59, 62, 70, 80, 84, 106
Calineuria californica, 128
Callibaetis, 15-16, 42, 61, 97-99, 126
Callibaetis nigritus, 97, 126
Callibaetis Partridge Spinner, 130
Callibaetis Swimming Nymph, 98, 132
Cased Caddis Larva, 74, 132
catch and release regulations, 138
Cave Falls, 47
Chernobyl Ant, 132
Chester Backwater, 41-42
Cheumatopsyche campyla, 77, 80, 128
Chief Joseph, 7
Chironomidae, 102
chokecherries, 38
Cicada, 111
Cinnamon Flying Ant, 131
Clouser Minnow, 53, 133
Coffee Pot Area, 12-14
Coffee Pot Campground, 14
Coffee Pot Rapids, 13, 14, 64, 91
Conehead Bugger, 19, 133
Conehead Rabbit Leech, 133
Copper John Nymph, 133

craneflies, 101
crayfish, 18, 121, 133
cricket, 111
cripple patterns, 15, 85, 89, 100, 130
Crowe Beetle, 131
cutthroat, 6, 11, 37, 45, 62

damselflies, 10, 14, 17, 61, 128
Dancing Caddis, 80, 131
Danskin, Jim, 91
Dave's Hopper, 111, 131
Deep Emergent Sparkle Pupa, 74
Deep Sparkle Pupa, 57, 132
deer flies, 101
Dennis, Jack, 67
dewatering, 138
Dinsmore Company, 116
Diphetor hageni, 82, 126
Diptera, 101, 128
Diving Blue-Winged Olive Egg Layer, 83, 133, 134
Diving Caddis, 75, 133
Double Bunny, 133
Double Wing, 44
double-fly rig, 69-70
Dr. Bar Emerger, 131
drift boats, 22, 35-36, 63, 90, 115
dropper fishing, 10, 23, 39, 44-46, 57, 62, 66-67, 69-70, 76, 77, 84-88, 100, 103, 111, 115-116
Drunella flavilinea, 95, 126
Drunella grandis, 88, 126
Dun Variant, 132

E-Z Caddis, 75, 131
Edmunds, George, 85
egg patterns, 13, 54
Elk Hair Caddis, 75-76, 118, 131
Emergent Sparkle Pupa, 10, 74, 76, 131, 134
Enallagma species, 128

Ephemerella grandis, 58
Ephemerella inermis, 1, 58, 81, 85, 126
Ephemerella simulans, 91, 126

Fall River, 45, 47-48, 64, 94, 109
Fall River Electric Cooperative, 19
Federal Energy Regulatory Commission, 19-20, 46
FERC. *See* Federal Energy Regulatory Commission.
Firehole River, 108-109
fish ladders, 19, 46, 138
Fishing Henry's Lake, by Bill Schiess, 10
Flasha-Bugger, 133
Flat Ranch, 11-12
Flav, 42, 95-96
Flesh Fly, 13
Flint, Oliver, ix, 73
float fishing, 24, 32-35
float tubing, 7, 9, 17
Floating Damsel, 10, 132
Floating Emergent Sparkle Pupa, 10
Floating Marabou Single Egg, 10
Floating Nymph, 132
floating line, 19, 114-115, 123
Fluttering Stone, 21, 131
Foam Ant, 108, 131
Foam Cicada, 131
forage fish, 14-15, 18, 25, 121
Forest Service, 25, 30, 35, 47, 48
Free-Living Caddis Larva, 74, 132

Gates, Cal, 75
Girdle Bug, 44, 45, 133
Glo Bug, 133
gnats, 101
Goff, Bill, 5
Gold-Ribbed Hare's Ear, 74, 89, 117, 120, 133

Golden Stone, 18, 21, 36, 70-71, 128
Goofus, 132
goose hunting, 29
Grand Targhee Ski Area, 53
Grand Tetons, 122, 125
Grandview Campground, 35
Grannom, 41, 55-56, 126
grasshoppers, 60, 108-111
Gray Drake, 41-42, 44, 93-95, 126
Gray Hackle Midge, 131
Great Gray Spotted Sedge, 70
Green Caddis Larva, 117, 120
Green Drake, 13, 14, 27, 28, 41, 58-60, 88-91, 92, 95, 96, 126
Green Drake Cripple, 89, 130
Green Drake Nymph, 59, 117, 120, 132
Green Drake Wulff, 130
Green Sedge, 77
Griffith's Gnat, 103, 131

H & L Variant, 132
Half Back Emerger, 86, 100, 131, 135
Halloween Woolly Bugger, 133
Halo Midge Emerger, 103, 131
Hare's Ear, 54, 133
Harriman State Park, 2-3, 6, 17, 25-29, 40, 48, 50, 59-60, 57-58, 78, 80, 82-84, 87, 88, 90-91, 93, 98, 99, 105, 107-109, 111-113, 118, 119-120, 124, 138
Harriman, Averill, 25
Harriman, E. H., 25
Harriman, Roland, 25, 107
Harrop, René, 59
Hatchery Ford, 32, 33, 35
hatchery trout, 19-20, 40, 46, 47
Hebgen Lake, 14, 61
Helicopsyche borealis, 128
Hemingway, Jack, 75
Hemingway Special, 75, 77, 80, 131

Hen Wing Spinner, 130

Hendrickson, 84

Henry's Fork Cricket, 131

Henry's Fork Foundation, 19, 138-139

Henry's Fork Golden Stone, 71, 131, 135

Henry's Fork Hopper, 109-110, 111, 131, 135

Henry's Fork Lodge, 32

Henry's Fork Salmon Fly, 68, 131, 135

Henry's Fork Yellow Sally, 131

Henry's Fork, The, by Charles Brooks, 25

Henry's Lake, 6-12, 14, 16, 62, 128

Henry's Lake Dam, 10

Henry's Lake Outlet, 10-12

Henry's Lake State Park, 7

Henry, Andrew, 43

Henryville Special, 75, 131

HFF. *See* Henry's Fork Foundation.

high stick method, 22, 114

high water, 19, 22

hoppers. *See* grasshoppers.

Humpy, 44, 86, 118, 132

hydro dam, 19, 45

hydroelectric facilities, 138

Hydropsyche cockerelli, 76, 126

Hydropsyche occidentalis, 76, 126

Idaho Department of Fish and Game, 14-15, 36, 40, 51

IDFG. *See* Idaho Department of Fish and Game.

Improved Buzz Ball, 103, 131

Improved Sofa Pillow, 21, 68, 131

Irresistible, 106, 132

irrigation, 23, 44, 49

Island Park Dam, 16, 19, 22, 27, 45, 60, 133, 138

Island Park Reservoir, 6, 12, 14-17, 19-20, 57, 60-61, 88, 91, 98, 103, 133

Isoperla species, 128

Jackson Hole, Wyoming, 48, 53

Joe's Hopper, 110

Kaufmann Black Stone, 132

Kaufmann Scud, 133

Kaufmann's Stimulator, 68, 111, 131

Kiwi Muddler, 133

Kokanee Salmon, 13, 133

Krystal Bugger, 10, 133

LaFontaine, Gary, 72, 74

Lamm, Bob, 44

Last Chance, 27, 57-58, 76, 84, 87, 89, 95, 104

Lawson, Chris, 70, 124

Lawson Golden Stone, 132

Lawson, Mike, 138

Lawson, Rick, 52, 108-109

Lawson, Shaun, 50, 70, 124

Lawson, Sheralee, 35, 124

leeches, 10, 14, 18, 25, 60, 121

Letort Hopper, 110

Lilly, Bud, 91

Limestone Cripple, 130

Little Olive, 128, 131

Little Sister Sedge, 42, 77, 80, 128

Little Western Weedy Water Sedge, 77, 126

livestock grazing, 138

Long-Horn Sedge, 59, 77, 80, 128

low water, 16, 19, 23-24

Lower Mesa Falls, 32-33, 35, 36

Mack's Inn, 13, 14

Madam X, 132

Mahogany Dun, 42, 61, 99-100, 124, 126, 130
Manlove, William R., 138
Marabou Muddler, 133
Marinaro, Vince, 110
Martin, Kim, 39
Matuka, 133
mayflies, 1, 14-15, 18, 26-28, 41-43, 48-49, 50-51, 55, 57, 59, 62, 81-100, 114, 126-132
Mayfly Cripple, 130
Mesa Falls, 33, 47
Mesa Falls Scenic Highway, 47
midges, 15, 55, 101-104, 128
Mike's Brown Drake, 130
Mike's Gray Drake, 130
Mike's Green Drake, 130
minnows, 15, 121
Modern Dry Fly Code, A, by Vince Marinaro, 110
Mohair Leech, 133
mosquitoes, 101
Mother's Day Caddis, 56, 76
Muddler Minnow, 133
Mystacides alafimbriata, 80, 128

National Fish and Wildlife Foundation, 138
Nature Conservancy, 11-12
Neophylax rickeri, 128
Nez Perce, 7
No-Hackle, 31, 59, 85, 96, 99-100, 108, 130, 136
nymphs, 13, 17-18, 22-23, 60, 64-68, 83, 86-87, 91-92, 112, 125

Oecetis avara, 77, 128
Oecetis disjuncta, 77, 128
Ole Pro. *See* Pat Barnes.
Olive Humpy, 120
open space, 138

Osborne Bridge, 27, 29-31, 33, 76, 99
Osborne Spring, 29

Pale Cream Stone Fly Nymph, 132
Pale Morning Dun, 27, 30, 42, 48, 58, 81, 84-86, 88, 96, 107, 126
Parachute Adams, 42, 94, 98, 120, 132
Parachute Cricket, 111, 131
Parachute Hopper, 111, 131
Paradrake, 90, 92, 130
Paraleptophlebia bicornuta, 99, 126
Parker Highway Bridge, 43
Partridge Caddis Emerger, 74, 76, 80, 131
Peacock Caddis, 75, 131, 137
Peeking Caddis, 74, 132
Pheasant Tail, 23, 39, 54, 57, 114, 117, 120
Pheasant Tail Nymph, 39, 100, 133, 136
pine bark beetles, 132
Pinehaven, 29, 31, 87, 99
Pink Cahill Parachute, 85
PMD, 130-132, 81, 84
PMD. *See* Pale Morning Dun
Pond's Lodge, 33, 46
Pontoon Hopper, 110
pontoon boat, 63
presentation, 4, 26, 110
Prince Nymph, 23, 26, 39, 54, 57, 117, 120, 133, 137
Pseudocloeon edmundsi, 82
Pteronarcys californica, 128

Quill Gordon, 84, 131, 84

rainbows, 6, 14, 20, 37, 40, 45, 47, 48, 53, 54, 59, 61, 62, 71, 82, 87, 106, 124, 133

Ranunculus, 78
Rapala, 20
reach cast, 119
Red Quill, 131
Renegade, 26, 40, 74, 88, 103, 120, 132
Rexburg, 39, 45, 49, 60
Rhyacophila bifida, 77
Richards, Carl, 31, 85
Rithrogena morrisoni, 55, 83, 126
Riverside, 29, 32-33
Riverside Campground, 32, 76
Robinson Creek, 33, 37
Rocky Mountain Whitefish, 49
rotenone, 14
Royal Trude, 120, 132
Royal Wulff, 3, 26, 44, 88, 103, 118, 120, 132
Rubber Legs Nymph, 19
Rusty Hen Spinner, 100, 137

Salmon Flies, 13, 18, 21, 35, 37, 38, 42, 55, 57-58, 63-71, 128
Schiess, Bill, 9
Schroeder, Ed, 111
Schwiebert, Ernie, 78
sculpins, 18, 121
Selective Trout, by Doug Swisher and Carl Richards, 31, 85
Serendipity, 74, 102, 133
Sheep Falls, 33, 35
shrimp, 10, 14
Shroud, 15, 98, 131
sight fishing, 113-114
Silver Creek, 98
sink-tip line, 8, 19, 56, 123
sinking line, 8-10, 16, 36, 62, 114, 123
Siphlonurus occidentalis, 94, 126
Skating Spider, 132
slot limits, 138

Small Western Green Drake, 95, 126
Smithsonian Institution, ix, 73
Snake River, 43
Snow Fly, 104, 131
South Fork Snake River, ix, 6, 36, 85, 94
Sparkle Duns, 130
Sparkle Pupa, 10, 57, 74, 76, 131-132, 134
spawning, 7, 19, 37-38, 40, 45, 46, 53-54, 62
Speckled Peter, 128
Speckled Spinner, 97, 126
Spent Partridge Caddis, 75, 77-78, 131, 137
split shot, 84, 115-116, 123
Spotted Sedge, 42, 59, 70, 76-77, 126
spring runoff, 38, 44, 48, 55, 57, 76
spring, 55-57
St. Anthony, 40, 41, 42, 45, 52-54, 60, 76, 84, 95, 99, 104
Staley Springs, 7
Stimulator, 38, 68, 111, 120, 131-132
stoneflies, 18-19, 21, 23, 38, 57, 63, 66-68, 76, 128
streamers, 13, 19-20, 35, 53, 56, 62, 121-125
strike indicators, 22-23, 112-115
Sugar City, 48-49
summer, 57-61
Sun Valley, 53
Surprise Falls, 35
Swisher, Doug, 31, 85

tailwaters, 3, 40, 52,
Targhee Forest, 33
terrestrials, 38, 60, 62, 105-111
Teton Dam, 48
Teton River, 45, 48-49, 109
Thorax Dun, 82, 85, 96, 99, 100, 130

Tiny Blue-Winged Olive, 82, 126
tippet, 5, 88, 97, 119-120, 124
Traverso, Dom, 86
Trico, 42, 48, 61, 81, 86-88, 99, 126
Tricorythodes minutus, 81, 86, 126
Triple Bar X, 69, 131
Troth, Al, 75
Trout Unlimited, 36
Trude, 38, 44, 132
Trumpeter Swans, 98
Turck's Tarantula, 68, 70, 132
two-fly rig, 62, 56, 84

University of Utah, 85
Upper Mesa Falls, 34, 35
Utah Chub, 14

Variegated Midge Larva, 102, 133
Vernon Bridge, 40
Victor, 48

wading, 17, 24, 29, 40, 44-45, 69
Warm River, 32, 33, 35-38, 46-47
weed beds, 16, 17, 60, 62, 78-79, 87
Weedy Water Sedge, 77-78, 126
Wendall Bridge, 39
West End Campground, 17, 103
West Yellowstone, Montana, 66, 115
Western Green Drake, 88, 91, 126
Western March Brown, 55, 83-84, 126
white water, 33-35, 36
whitefish, 37, 49-51, 92-93, 124
Whitlock Damsel, 132
Whitlock, Dave, 112
Wild Thing theory, 26
wild trout, 19-20, 47, 48
wind, 16, 27-28, 95-97, 108-110
winter, 52-55, 104
Wood Road #16, 27, 30, 31, 86
Wood Road #6, 33

Wool Head Sculpin, 19, 133
Woolly Bugger, 10, 56, 69, 133
Woolly Worm, 10, 133
www.henrysfork.com, 139
Wyethia, 79

yarn, 134, 23, 56, 76
Yellow Sally, 38, 128
Yellowstone National Park, 32, 47-48, 94, 108-109, 115
Yellowstone River, 56
yo-yo method, 10
Young, Tom, ix
Yuk Bug, 44, 133

Z-lon, 89, 100, 108
Zonker, 19, 53, 56, 124, 133

ABOUT THE AUTHORS

IKE LAWSON

Born and raised on Idaho's Henry's Fork River, Mike Lawson has fished it from its source down to its confluence with the South Fork of the Snake River—almost one hundred miles of some of the finest trout fishing in the country.

According to Lawson, this river offers more diversity of water types than any other river in the world. In *Fly Fishing the Henry's Fork*, he shares the experience and wisdom he has accumulated in more than forty years of fishing and observing this acclaimed waterway.

Lawson owned and operated the Henry's Fork Anglers fly shop for twenty-two years, is published in *Fly Fisherman, American Angler*, and *Trout Magazine*, and, along with his wife Sheralee, is an active member of the Henry's Fork Foundation that works to improve and protect the river. At home near the river, Lawson fishes it year-round and is also an avid bird hunter.

ARY LAFONTAINE

Though not as continuously, noted fly fisher and award-winning author Gary LaFontaine has fished the Henry's Fork River for twenty-plus years and spent one season on the river collecting insects for the hatch charts in his landmark book, *Caddisflies*.

His other acclaimed books include *The Dry Fly: New Angles, Trout Flies: Proven Patterns*, and *Fly Fishing the Mountain Lakes*, and he has written innumerable magazine articles for fly-fishing publications. Named Angler of the Year in 1996 by *Fly Rod & Reel*, he is currently a columnist for *Trout Magazine*, contributing editor to *Fly Rod & Reel*, and star of several fly-fishing videos. He lives in Montana with his famous fly-fishing dog, Chester, and his ruins-the-fishing Rottweiler, Zeb.